SECULAR CHRISTIANITY

SECULAR CHRISTIANITY

Ronald Gregor Smith

78901

HARPER & ROW PUBLISHERS

New York and Evanston

FIRST EDITION

LIBRARY OF CONGRESS CATALOG CARD NUMBER: 66-20785

To
the President Dr Arthur R. McKay
the Faculty and Students
of
McCormick Theological Seminary
Chicago
in gratitude for a happy semester
September 1964–January 1965

Preface

This book came into being as a course of lectures delivered at McCormick Theological Seminary, Chicago, during the winter semester September 1964 to January 1965, when I had the privilege of being Visiting Professor in residence at that hospitable and distinguished Seminary. The dedication seeks to express formally the gratitude of my wife and myself for all the kindness we experienced during those months.

Parts of what I have to say were also presented at the Southern Methodist University, Dallas, Texas, where I recall especially the sympathetic encouragement of Professor Schubert M. Ogden, and at the Colgate-Rochester Divinity School, Rochester, New York, where the President, Dr Gene Bartlett, and the Faculty members, in particular Professor William Hamilton, made a brief week's visit a happy and memorable occasion for us.

The list of books at the end indicates the immediate background to my reflections. It is not intended as a complete bibliography. Moreover, in the interval between writing and publication one or two other works have appeared, or come to my notice, which would certainly deserve fuller mention in a more comprehensive study. Harvey Cox's *The Secular City* is one example. Another is E. L. Mascall's *The Secularization of Christianity*. But, as a sensitive reader should quickly learn from a perusal of Professor Mascall's book, English scholars have still a long way to go before they are able to enter into the new discussion with a positive appreciation of the issues involved. It is chiefly to the Continent, and to a lesser extent to the United States, that we must at present look for creative contributions to the revolution which is overtaking reflection about faith in the modern secular world.

That there is such a revolution, and that we stand today at the threshold of what may be a real step forward in the understanding and practice of Christian faith, is the under-lying theme of what I have attempted here. Faith in the context of history, history as qualified by the reality of Christ as *the* eschatological event, and secularity as the real possibility offered by the reality of Christ—these are the interlocking themes which provide, as it seems to me, the ground for a new view of the liberating powers which are to be found in Christianity. And it is in these liberating powers that I believe it is possible to hope for unprecedented changes in the style and the practice of faith.

But this is not a time for systems of theology, or for a parade of assurance. Theology cannot consist of pronouncements, but must rather hope to provide a contribution to the dialogue about our common human predicament.

For those who are interested in such matters it should be added that I regard this book as a development of my earlier essay, *The New Man* (1956) : a development rather than a sequel. For it develops certain consequences of what I said there, and clarifies and modifies other things. In particular, I have tried to face the paradoxical reality of the event of Christ in history as both the end and the beginning of history : the end of all old hopes, iconoclastic and death-bringing, and the beginning of a new hope which is thoroughly secular. This is the depth of the eschatological reality of Christ's life and death.

PREFACE

I have of course consistently tried to give references, not only for quotations but also for ideas, to the many writers from whom I have learned. But there is one in particular whose thoughts have become so much a part of my own views that I can scarcely disentangle them from mine : Professor Rudolf Bultmann of Marburg, who through a long lifetime of devotion to the truth has always been so immensely generous in help to those who seek it, and quick and sensitive in his encouragement.

Most of the actual writing was done in Kronshagen in Holstein, at the home of my sister-in-law, Frau Annelise Schulze-Rolfshörn, then in Rengsdorf in the Rhineland, at the home of Dr and Mrs Eberhard Bethge, and finally in the summer-house in the Eifel of Professor Max Graf zu Solms. It is a pleasure to record my gratitude to these friends for their hospitality and forbearance during these happy months.

One formal acknowledgement has to be made, and that is to the Seabury Press of New York, for some sentences taken from my own essay on 'Post-Renaissance Man', contributed to a symposium entitled *Conflicting Images of Man*, edited by William Nicholls, to be published January 1966

R. G. S.

Leversbach, Eifel

Contents

4. *Faith as personal* 39

Faith is personal, which means more than an individual matter, but the emergence of the personal I over against his Thou, to which he is summoned by God. This I now lives in the world realized as a personal reality

5. *Faith as a unity in relation* 44

Faith as a unity in relation of the Giver of faith and the believer. The traditional divisions, whether of *notitia*, *assensus*, *fiducia*, or subject and object, cannot comprehend the historical complexity of God's gracious act

6. *Faith as justification* 47

This gracious act, so far as the self-understanding of faith is concerned, offers a new possibility in man's relation to God and to the world. This is the possibility of sonship. Man's justification means that he is accepted by God as having come of age.

7. *Faith not an empirical phenomenon* 53

Faith is not an observable empirical phenomenon, and its fruits are not objects in the world which we may use as proofs of the meaning of faith or as a vindication of meaning in history

8. *Faith and the traditional arguments for God's existence* 59

The traditional 'proofs' of God's existence are not proofs. There is no immediacy of God in history. Faith recognizes the world as empty of gods, and of God. Only in faith as a historical response to God's act in history may God be encountered

II. HISTORY

1. Introduction 67

The concept of history has become the central one in theology. This links with the centrality of Christ as the term by which we seek to understand the reality of God's relation to man. It points to the reality itself, in which God and man come together. The modern approach to the theme of history arose in biblical criticism, and the true authority of Christianity came to be recognized as the reality of history itself

CONTENTS

CONTENTS

III. SECULARISM

1. Introduction 135

The present powers of secularism as a widespread technological dynamism

2. The history of the term 'secular' 141

The history of the term 'secularism' in Europe down to the Jerusalem Missionary Conference

3. The source of secularism 150

The source of secularism in Christian faith. Faith lets the world be itself. Christ himself is truly secular, living entirely by faith, i.e. entirely freely for the world and entirely freely for God. In this faith concerning Christ the world is liberated

4. The ambiguity of secularism 157

Secularism will not recognize its sources, and the possibility of its renewal. And it refuses to be radically and consistently secular. It replaces man by an ideology or by nihilism. It refuses the real autonomy offered to it by a radical faith

5. Faith not religion 175

Faith itself is caught up in the ambiguity of secularism. It confuses itself with religion. Religion is the attempt to use God as a completion to man's life

6. God-language 186

God-language is still possible, *pace* van Buren, in terms of the acknowledgement of a claim upon our lives rising out of history. God is transcendent in the midst of history, and in the midst of our lives. God is fully historical being

7. Secular Christianity 194

or the style of faith

EPILOGUE 205

Prayer as the existence of eschatological faith, or the anticipation of the End

LIST OF BOOKS 213

INDEX 217

Introduction

During my preparations for this course of lectures on *Secular Christianity* I tried to keep before my mind's eye the image of a modern man. At first it was a kaleidoscopic image, shifting and uncertain. For it is not easy to have enough sympathy and historical imagination to get past one's own self-understanding. In one sense this is neither desirable nor possible. But gradually the image became more distant, and also clearer, and the picture settled down, and I could see the lineaments without difficulty. Certainly, this meant an assumption, and a decision, about what and who is a modern man. The propriety of this assumption and this decision will have to be judged by all that I have to say. At least it should be clear that no one can begin without tying a knot somewhere.

The background for my image of modern man is the Germany of the pre-war years, and then of the Third Reich and the brutality and terror of the Nazi régime. At first many figures claimed my attention: the simple Protestant pastor, Paul Schneider, who died in a concentration camp before the war began;[1] the mighty figure of Karl Barth, refusing to give the oath of loyalty to Hitler, and leaving his chair in Bonn University to return, in the end, to his

[1] The story of Paul Schneider is told by his widow in a little book entitled *Der Prediger von Buchenwald*.

15

native Switzerland; Pastor Niemöller, whose long imprisonment turned him practically into a symbol and legend of
heroic Christian resistance during his lifetime; Dietrich
Bonhoeffer, whose letters from prison have become a
turning-point in modern theology, and who is now in
danger of being idolized by a new generation of students
who did not know him; and many others, politicians,
lawyers, priests, professors, scientists, students, and simple
people.

The figure who stands in my mind for all these is a German
aristocrat, landowner and lawyer, Helmut James Graf von
Moltke, born in Kreisau in Mecklenburg in 1907, hanged
in January 1945 in Tegel prison in Berlin. He came of
a famous family, his father being one of the great German
generals of the first world war, and his grand-uncle the
head of the German army during the Franco-Prussian war.
But his own fame does not rest on any military achievement.
In fact, though he was one of the leading figures in the
resistance to Hitler, and was in the end hanged because of
his complicity in the conspiracy against Hitler, he was
opposed to any plot of assassination. He did not believe
that the hopes for the future of Germany and of a Christian
Europe could be realized upon the foundation of an act of
violence. His fame, to my mind, rests not so much upon
any actions which he undertook, or refused to undertake,
in his resistance to Hitler, as simply upon what he was in
himself. And what he was can be read in a tiny book of
letters, in fact upon just two letters which he wrote to his
wife, and managed to smuggle out of prison while he was
awaiting the inevitable sentence of death.

From these letters I quote just a few sentences:
I do not in the least have the feeling that has sometimes overcome me, that I should like to see everything
just once more. But neither do I feel at all 'other-

worldly'. You see that I am happy as I talk to you,
instead of turning to God. There is a hymn with the
words, 'For he who holds in life to thee is ready to die'.
That is exactly how I feel. Since I am alive today
I must hold in life to him; he does not ask for more.
Is that Pharisaic? I do not know. But I believe that
I do know that now I live in his grace and forgiveness,
and have nothing and do nothing of myself . . . I do
not concern myself with God or with my death. He
has the inexpressible grace to come to me and to
concern himself with me.[1]

In these words we have, it seems to me, a picture of the
modern man of the kind that anticipates and realizes all
that we may hope for. He is a man of faith, and at the
same time he is a man fully in this world. He does not
feel at all other-worldly, and he is quite happy writing to
his wife instead of turning consciously to God. He does not
go to God, he does not need to go to God, for God in his
inexpressible grace has come to him. So he lives in the
world, acts and joins in the responsibilities of the world,
and yet he is sovereign over the world. He lives in the
dialectic of faith which connects him simultaneously to God
and to the world. In this extraordinary situation he is
even able to smile when the President of the Nazi Court,
Herr Freisler, is indulging in one of his worst tirades.
His face turned as red as his robes, said Moltke in his
letter to his wife, and there could not be more upheaval
if a man were to jump into the crocodile pond in the
Zoo.

I should like to keep this image of Moltke in his last
days before us. He was not a theologian, and in most ways
he was a quiet and unostentatious man, happiest when he
was looking after his estate and trying to make it pay. The

[1]Helmut James Graf von Moltke, *Letzte Briefe*, Berlin 1950, pp. 49*f*, 52.

pictures which have survived of him, standing before the
judges in the court in Berlin, show a tall, fine, intellectual,
somewhat remote person, who has already suffered much
physically from prolonged imprisonment, and spiritually
from the assault upon his beliefs, a man with a cool glance
who does not invite easy friendship: but at the same time
a man who walks in utter fearlessness, and composure,
even relaxation, in his faith.

He represents the hope of Christianity. In the grim and
even apocalyptic situation of the Nazi régime in Germany
the outlines of such a man are as it were etched in sharp
relief. It was a time of decisions which were fraught with
destiny, not only for Germany, not only for Europe, but
for the whole future history of mankind. But Moltke, and
others with him, stand as more than symbols: they
were actual living men who lived out in their actions
and their sufferings the possibilities of Christian faith in our
time.

This then is the picture which is so to speak the motto
for my theological reflections. Into whatever abstract fields
we may be led, at least the intention is clear: I wish to
understand how we may look at our inheritance, and how
we may face our future, in the strength and the inspiration
of such a man as Helmut James Graf von Moltke. On the
view of theology and of history which I wish to elaborate
here, such a man is one of the real makers of history. For
it is only in relation to historical action that faith, and
reflection about faith, which is the business of theology,
take on their authentic nature. Both faith and theology
involve commitment of some kind. Faith which is exhausted
in words is idle chatter; and theology whose concepts are
related only to one another in a realm of ideas or values is
less than a spider's web, for at least the web is the spider's
parlour.

I am not saying that theology is not also a matter of concepts. Far less do I wish to suggest that theology is identical with proclamation or preaching. But through its connexion with the substance of faith, and through the deepening and strengthening of faith in its turn by the reflective work of theology, there arises the possibility of a truly theological faith. It is only when this possibility is actively present that both preaching, in the technical sense, and theology, in the sense of a system of rational concepts, are able to move out of the rarefied atmosphere of the professional Christian circles. For then there underlies them both, and sustains them, a faith which is seen primarily as historical existence.

The intricate connexions and mutual influences which are at work here will be more apparent when we enter into the actual material of our reflections. But I should like to offer here some indication in advance of the way that I hope we may go.

If it were possible to think of the territory we are about to traverse as being supplied in advance with a map, then I should suggest that the title of the map might be 'Christianity as history'. Then theology would be the path we are going to take across this land. Unfortunately, however, there is no ready-made path, and no map. For each generation has to find its own path, and use its own landmarks. Theology is not something eternally fixed and ready-made. For though theology certainly works with concepts, it does not find them ready to hand as ideal constructs. But they are always related to the actual territory, and this means that they are always in movement. A static theology would at once lose touch with the historicity of Christianity which is its life-reference. Theological concepts are always relative to Christian history. They are shifting all the time, because they are in time and not in eternity. Theology is not a system of timeless truths, but a description of what goes on in Christianity.

An immediate objection to this view is easy to make. It is this: surely theology, as the word strictly indicates, is the science of God, or the study of God: how then can we claim to speak of God in terms of a shifting and relative description? And surely the path of Christianity is clearly marked on the map of tradition? There are guides and authorities, landmarks, standards, momentous acts—in fact the map is crowded with aids to a straight journey. Orthodoxy, or right opinion, the rule of faith for understanding and living—is this not to be found by the simple application of the received truth? And even though there are domestic differences, even disputes, about which is the right path, especially at certain turning-points on the journey, is the general direction not clearly and unalterably fixed? We have the Bible, we have the early creeds and councils, we have the later confessions and standards of the church in its various parts; in brief, the whole massive and subtle complex of the tradition.

In all this, is there not an absoluteness which rises authoritatively above the shifting and relative circumstances of our lives? In fact, this objection might be summarized in terms of the absoluteness of God, his absolute demand upon us, and by contrast our incapacity to break out of our subjective whimsies and get anywhere on this journey without simple and unbroken obedience to this absoluteness. For is not God above all relativity and change, without beginning, or process, or end? And if we speak of him in any other terms are we not just deluding ourselves? Are we not then just talking about ourselves, about man and not God? Is my theological journey not in danger of being transformed into an anthropological excursion, motivated by man's self-concern rather than controlled by the map of God's demands?

Now my answer to this objection is not one that I can produce as easily as the objection itself. For there is indeed a real and important truth in the objection. It is the truth, so simple and yet so hard, that God is not the world. Nor is he man. Between God and the world, and between God and man, there is an infinite qualitative difference. God is wholly different from man. Between God and man there is a gulf which man cannot bridge.

But this truth can never be put forward as a merely formal axiom. Nor indeed in its long history in Christian thought—long before Kierkegaard or Karl Barth made it so pivotal for their thought—has it ever been entirely disconnected from the historical realities of faith. As the problem of the absolutely unconditioned and its relation to the relative and conditioned, it appears, of course, in other connexions. In the connexion of faith we need only say here that what has been traditionally called God's transcendence involves a truth which we cannot yield. At the same time it is a truth which is always in danger of being distorted when taken by itself, or when understood in terms of categories other than those which arise out of the consideration of faith.

In our time it seems to me that Christian faith points to another way of talking about the absoluteness or the transcendence of God. The sub-title of my as yet *carta rasa* might be 'God's history with man', or, even more simply, 'the history of God'. For this, it seems to me, is the form which the audacious claim of Christian faith takes in our time, that what it, Christian faith, has to do with is God in history, more precisely, God's existence as history, God's historicity. And for the journey we have now to take we have to sketch our map as we go. Our theological conceptions, our standards and authorities, have to be examined in the context of a journey which is necessarily different from all other journeys, for the simple reason that our time, like every time, has its own unique problems and possibilities. And these may be summed up in the affirmation of faith that we have to do with God in history and nowhere else.

I. FAITH

1. Faith as historical

I ended my preliminary remarks by saying that faith has to do with God in history. I want now to examine this statement, especially in its implications for the meaning of faith. My other main themes, history and secularism, can of course not be excluded, but I shall examine them more closely later.

I am speaking here specifically of Christian faith. This elision has historical roots, to the extent that in the early church Christian faith very rapidly came to be described simply as faith, even as *the* faith, or, as we might say, faith *par excellence*. Thus we hear Stephen described in the Book of Acts as 'a man full of faith',[1] and we hear St Paul exhorting the new disciples 'to continue in the faith'.[2] A characteristic late formulation is found in the Epistle of Jude, verse 3, where we hear of 'the faith once for all delivered to the saints'.

Now this is not just a sign of intolerance on the part of the early Christians, as though they imagined that they alone knew what faith was. And even if we deplore the danger, inherent in this development, of a certain hardening of the term, which was later to lead to the institutionalising of faith as equivalent to subscription to a formula, there is another and altogether more dynamic interpretation possible. Certainly, it would be wrong to try to reserve the term

[1]Acts 6.5.   [2]Acts 14.22.

25

'faith', or 'believing', for the Christian situation. The word 'faith' can be used in other contexts. For instance, there is a perfectly sensible meaning in the sentence, 'I believe in so-and-so.' Again, a physicist has good justification for saying that he 'believes' in the regularity of nature when he makes, and then repeats, an experiment. And I do not think that we have any right to deprive adherents of other religions of the use of this word 'faith' and its cognates.

But the early use of this word 'faith' in Christian history in what is almost a technical sense indicates a more positive but not necessarily an exclusive claim. Faith is co-terminous with all that Christianity is. Christianity is faith. That is to say, faith is essentially historical.

This historicity of faith contains two distinct elements. First, faith is historical in the sense that it arises as the consequence of certain events in history, and second, these historical events constitute the shape and content of faith.

First, faith arises as the consequence of certain events in history. These events are concentrated in the revelatory act of God in his Word. This Word which is revealed is Christ. But because this Word is God's revelatory act in history, it is not to be grasped, nor is it properly understood, when it is regarded merely as an object awaiting our understanding. This Word is not just a declaration, or a statement. When we say that the Word of God is a revelatory act in history we are saying that it is something more than, and different from, a proposition about God's purpose or his nature. Of course it is possible, and even necessary, to draw certain inferences about God's purpose and nature from this revelatory situation. But the heart of the situation is not an idea which we infer from a declaration, however illuminating.

Even if you were to suggest that God's revelation in his Word is that he is love, then I should be inclined to ask

whether you are not in danger of abstracting an idea from
the living historical revelation. It is in the context of this
danger that I accept the intention, though not necessarily
the consequences, of Mr Gerald Downing's recent study of
the meaning of revelation.[1] In spite of the danger, however,
I think we may still use the concept of revelation, provided
we understand it in terms which imply its historical dynamism. Thus we may still consider ourselves entitled to repeat
the words, 'God is love', as a pointer to the revelatory
situation. But these words are not in that case used in the
sense of a timeless idea, above all change, untouched by its
historical context, unconnected with our own commitment
to it. But the context and the commitment remain an
integral part of the affirmation, as they are an integral
part of the revelatory act.

This becomes clearer when we ask what we really mean
by saying that God reveals himself in Christ as love. Love
is a highly complex concept, and in the situation of God's
act in Christ towards men it is at once refracted into various
forms. As soon as we face this affirmation in its historical
context we are drawn into the situation in such a way that
the affirmation as it were breaks into life: there is demand,
there is judgment, there is forgiveness. Forgiveness for what
we are may be taken, for the present, as the best summary of
the historical reality of God's loving act in Christ. So faith
may therefore be described as acceptance of this forgiveness.
In Bultmann's words, 'faith is obedient submission to God's
revelation in the word of proclamation.' So faith does
not merely follow upon, but it is the direct consequence of,
the historical message of God in Christ.

But second, the content and shape of faith are constituted
by the historical events. Faith takes its content as well as

[1] *Has Christianity a Revelation?* Library of Philosophy and Theology,
1964.

its form from the content and form of God's historical act. To live in faith means to live by faith in that historical Word which both demands your response and effects in you God's liberating forgiveness. You cannot acquire faith, as something that henceforth belongs to you, and that you possess, whether in the form of a certain feeling about God (an 'experience'), or in the form of a certainty which once it is acquired can dispense with its source. But faith remains bound to the events which gave rise to it. It remains a matter of historical commitment. It is not simply that you have to return to the source of faith in order to refresh it (though this too plays a necessary part) as that when faith is cut loose from that source it simply loses its reality. Faith is not a phenomenon in the world which is capable of pursuing an independent existence either in the world of objects or in the 'inwardness' of the subject. There are many views of faith which fall short of the reality, or mistakenly identify it with a certain kind of individualism or mysticism, because they wish to classify it either as something 'objective' or something 'subjective'. In both cases the attempt is made to regard faith as an object, whether confined to some eccentric individuals or to an esoteric 'mystical' realm which is also the preserve of some individuals. On the contrary, faith is historical through and through, and is determined by its relation to the historical reality of Christ.

So in these two ways, in the historical context of God's action as originative and as the constantly recurring call for commitment, faith is to be described as essentially and eminently historical.

2. *What faith is not*

The use of the word 'historical' in describing faith is still, admittedly, in need of closer definition. We may be helped towards a definition by seeing what faith does *not* imply.

It does not imply a metaphysical scheme. It does not imply a mythological world-view. And it does not imply a moralistic standpoint. Let us take each of these negatives in turn.

First, it does not imply a metaphysical scheme. By this I mean a view of the world which has been arrived at independently of the historical commitment of faith. This can take many different forms, in accordance with the particular frame of any period of history. The characteristic form in the early days of Christianity was the gnostic. Gnosis, or Gnosticism, is an elusive entity, similar in this respect to the generalized idea of science and a scientific attitude, better, scientism, which is so powerful today. Like scientism, too, Gnosticism was so pervasive that it was widely accepted almost as the natural or inevitable point of view. For these reasons it is difficult to determine just precisely what it did involve.

In the Gnostic view of life there was certainly a radical dualism. The world and matter were evil, and hostile to God. The way of salvation lay through an escape from the powers of the world into the hands of God. The world was darkness, and the realm of light could only be reached by an utter denial of this evil world. The means of escape lay along the way of special initiation, by means of gnosis or knowledge, into the quite distinct realm of God. In this realm the 'principalities and powers' were helpless.

It is possible to regard these views as representing primarily a metaphysic, that is, a view of the cosmos which implies an attitude of being. This is the interpretation I adopt, following in the main the interpretation given by Hans Jonas. Jonas speaks of the Gnostic cosmology as asserting 'a radical difference between human life and the life of the world outside man'.[1] Thus the Gnostic view was expressed in 'an immense uncertainty of being, in a world-*angst, angst* in face of the world and *angst* at oneself'.[2] The knowledge which Gnosticism offered of the self and of God was thus further to be described as entirely non-worldly, in the sense both of unworldly and anti-worldly.

Others have tended to see in Gnosticism simply a heresy within Christianity. This is unlikely. The basic metaphysical starting-point of Gnosticism is quite different from the historical starting-point of Christian faith. There is a realism in Christian faith which is not to be found in Gnostic views. Christian faith does not start from a philosophical perception or a cosmological insight, but from man's actual situation in the world. Certainly, like Gnosticism, Christianity recognizes the evil in the world and the hostility of the world to God. In these respects it bears a certain resemblance to Gnosticism, in its consequent dualist tendency. But this dualism in Christianity is not thorough-going, for the source of the trouble in the world is not seen as due to a cosmic misfortune but to man's own sin. And the resolution of man's predicament, according to Chris-

[1]Hans Jonas, *Gnosis und Spätantiker Geist*, I, Göttingen, 1934, p. 170.
[2]*ibid.*, p. 143.

tianity, does not lie in denying the world to be God's, but in affirming God's unchanging goodness.

Others again have been more impressed with the mythological aspects of Gnosticism, especially with its personifying and allegorizing tendencies. The difference between a metaphysical scheme and a mythological world-view is nevertheless a real one, even though it is clear that in Gnosticism the basic metaphysical view is expressed in a great variety of ways, including mythological forms.

There are clearer instances in the story of Christendom of what I should call metaphysical intervention, even domination. But precisely the lack of clarity in the story of the relationship between Gnosticism and Christian faith in the early generations of Christendom indicates the seriousness of the problem which faces Christian faith: the problem of self-understanding, and self-expression, in terms of its own historical existence, and not in terms borrowed from an alien view of the world.

Not all instances of the relationship between Christianity and a metaphysic can be described simply as unfortunate. For example, the great effort of the middle ages to establish a strong and stable Christendom was one of the magnificent achievements of man's spirit. Essentially what was being sought there was a harmonization of the Aristotelian categories of thought with Hebrew prophetic faith. Out of this effort there arose a precarious harmony, expressed in the massive structure of Thomist theology, in which the clearly defined spheres of nature and of supernature were dovetailed together in one grand system. The cathedrals of the middle ages, and the *Divina Commedia* of Dante, may be regarded as reflections in the realm of art of that theology: with their foundations strong and firm in the earth and in historical and empirical experience, and their pinnacles soaring to heaven. In this balance between the absolute and the relative, between God and the world, it was indeed the metaphysic which predominated. Yet there were always powerful elements of Christian historical realism at play.

From this example we may conclude that Christian faith cannot avoid tensions, or an attempted harmony, with metaphysical views. It is even possible that this may happen again and again in the future, in forms of struggle as yet unknown to us.

Nevertheless, we must hold firmly to the affirmation that Christianity, or, more precisely, Christian faith, is not and never can be primarily a view of the world. It is a historical reality which carries its own understanding of God and man and the world within itself. And it cannot be identified with, or subsumed under, any philosophy, not even a philosophy of history. For what it produces out of itself is an understanding of itself, of the world and of God which is directly due to its own historicity. It is possible that this understanding by faith of its own historicity has a better chance in our time of finding radical non-metaphysical expression than ever before. One factor of great importance is the absence of any one dominant metaphysic. Since the Renaissance there has been a plurality of competing metaphysics, so that in this situation of fragmentation we are forced to ask more insistently than ever before whether the historicity of faith may not provide its own form and style of expression. This does not mean that we wish to supplant an understanding of the world, the self, and God by what Bonhoeffer called, with reference to Karl Barth's theology, 'positivism of revelation'. Rather, we wish to suggest a historical understanding which arises out of the historical existence of faith. What this involves in positive, concrete terms will appear later.

Secondly, faith does not imply a mythological world-view.

I should define a mythological world-view as a particular form of metaphysic in which a cosmology, that is, a view of the cosmos, is constructed out of objects in the empirical world. Such a mythology purports to talk about the other-worldly, about transcendence, in terms of this world. Its intention is to talk about man in relation to God. But it ends by turning this relationship, and with it both man and God, into objects in a pattern of thought. This location of man and God as objects in a pattern of thought becomes the dominant factor, and the historicity of faith vanishes. Neither the other-worldly which the mythology sought to grasp, nor the this-worldly which it sought to link with the other-worldly, is understood in its true nature.

It is ironical that Rudolf Bultmann's so-called 'demythologizing' of New Testament concepts has so widely been accused of 'dissolving' the historicity of Christianity. Precisely the opposite is Bultmann's clear intention—namely, to interpret Christian faith in terms of the historicity of the message concerning Christ. This fully historical interpretation demands a radical critique of the style of first-century thinking. This style is seen as primarily defective in its elision of historical reality with would-be 'objective' formulations. It is thus the loss of real transcendence which is the chief defect of this mythological style of thinking. For it involves thinking of God as an object who may be drawn into the scope of human understanding in a way similar to that in which objects in the world may be used and exploited.

If we speak of God in terms of mythological thought-patterns we turn him into a bit of the world, an extension of ourselves. The understanding of the self which is offered to us in Christian faith is the very opposite of this identification of God with ourselves or with the world. In other words, no mythological method can do justice to the con-

33

junction of sheer otherness with sheer grace which is the paradoxical style of the Christian message.

Lastly, the moralistic view of man in the world cannot contain faith. Here the matter is admittedly obscure, and a moralistic interpretation of faith has at times seemed to be entirely successful in overwhelming and eliminating the historicity of faith. Not only in the early days of Christianity, in the great struggle about the place of the law in Christian faith, but also at other great moments in Christian history, notably in the eighteenth century, the moralistic interpretation of faith has had great power. Nor is this surprising, when one remembers that even in St Paul, the great protagonist of the historicity of faith, the law is still affirmed as holy and just and good, as the custodian or tutor leading us to Christ.[1] There is a truth in the reality of the good will which we must not let go.

But, powerful though the moral element is in the experience of faith, it is not the straightforward control of faith. In the New Testament there is no doubt at all that the basic element is that the human will—and with it the man himself —is in the grip of evil. In other words, man's will is impotent to do the good. 'O wretched man that I am! Who shall deliver me from the body of this death?'[2] is the classic statement of the Pauline and the Christian position with regard to the will. Moreover, while it is a basic insight of Christian faith that the deliverance which man finds through God's forgiveness justifies him, or makes him righteous, this is something different from the straightforward movement of the good will leading a man to moral betterment. There is indeed a close and significant connexion between faith and man's whole relation to the world; but faith as essentially and pre-eminently historical is not circumscribed by the ethical demand.

[1]Romans 7.12; Galatians 3.24.   [2] See Romans 7.15–25.

3. Faith as free decision

When I say that faith as essentially and pre-eminently historical is not circumscribed by the ethical demand, I do not mean to detract from the moral reality of the decision of faith. Faith is a free decision on man's part, it is an act of his will in face of the historical demand of God in Christ. But this demand is not simple and sheer demand. It is simultaneously a gift. You are given forgiveness. Thus a relationship is established which cannot be adequately described in terms of the isolated will. 'Willed attentiveness' to your duty, as Professor Maclagan calls it,[1] is undoubtedly an element which may be abstracted from the complex situation of faith. But the whole situation is more rich and enigmatic than this analysis is capable of discerning. For the free decision of faith is always a response. And the call to which it is a response is the call to accept the forgiving and liberating Word of God. 'God be merciful to me a sinner'[2] strikes the authentic note of Christian faith. This is a truly paradoxical situation, for what we have now to say is that the response of faith is a free response, while at the same time it is the forgiving Word which sets us free.

How is this possible? Certainly, it is not possible to talk about forgiveness unless you have been forgiven. This might seem to close the discussion, and be a modern version of Tertullian's prescription of heretics. But it is possible to

[1] *The Theological Frontier of Ethics*, p. 169.   [2] Luke 18.13.

35

make a distinction here, which does not diminish the basic paradox, but still keeps open the discussion: while it is not possible to talk in terms of the actuality of forgiveness unless you have yourself experienced forgiveness, it is possible to *ask* about forgiveness before you have been forgiven. For unless you have some understanding of forgiveness before you accept it, you could not know it and accept it. But this understanding, as Professor Bultmann puts it so well, is different from rational explanation:

> I can understand what friendship, loyalty and love are; and precisely if I understand them aright I know the friendship, love and loyalty which are shown to me are always, and remain, a mystery which I thankfully accept. I do not grasp them by means of my rational thought, either by a logical deduction from the attitude of the others, or by psychological analysis, or by existential analysis, but only in the existential openness of my person for the encounter. In such openness I also understand what friendship, loyalty and love are, before they are given to me, since my existence needs them: I understand them in that case in the question concerning them. So I can also understand what God's grace means; otherwise I could not speak of it at all. But that this grace encounters me, that the gracious God is *my* God, is always a mystery, even in the revelation of it. But it is not a mystery because God is an irrational being or because he does something which pierces the course of the world in an incomprehensible manner, but because it is incomprehensible that he encounters me.[1]

In other words, all such intensely historical situations, forgiveness, friendship, love, involve something more than the isolated will, attentive to its duty. Primarily they are situa-

[1] *Kerygma und Mythos* II, p. 190.

tions in which there is give as well as take; there is mutuality of personal being, there is encounter.

This is more than the simple assertion of the will, and yet it includes this. But it includes it in such a way that there is a shift in the totality of your existence. Simultaneously with your utter responsibility you recognize and acknowledge your utter dependence. In friendship and in love, in regard to other human persons, there are always limitations upon this responsibility and this dependence. The chief limitation is posited by the fact that the responsibility and the dependence are reciprocal: there is inter-responsibility and interdependence between you and your friend, or you and your beloved, as it were on the same plane. If a man lays down his life for his friend, and later, in the course of that friend's continued life, it turns out that he did not understand the sacrifice, or did not act upon it in the fulness of the demand which it carried implicitly or explicitly with it—then what are we to say? Or if a man dies for the sake of a better world, if he volunteers, as so many did volunteer during the first world war, in a flush of idealism, to serve their country, and later it turns out that that country was ungrateful, or controlled by quite un-idealistic motives—then what are we to say?

I think we can only reiterate that upon every inter-human relationship there are bound to be limitations, from both sides of the relationship. And the absolute self-giving, in love or in friendship, is absolute only when it is related to the absolute, that is, to God. A sacrificial act may thus still be absolute, even in the relative situations of human responsibility and interdependence, if it reflects and expresses simultaneously the sense of absolute responsibility before God—'I must do this, no matter the consequences'—and the recognition of absolute dependence upon God. It is this latter recognition which lifts the action out of the realm of relative and partial ends, and gives it the substance of full historical existence before God. You act as a free man, and you are the servant of all men.

But this freedom and this service are not exhaustively defined in terms of the assertion of the individual will. Rather, the freedom is a freeing from the impotence of the isolated will ('For I do not do what I want, but I do the very thing I hate'[1]) by means of the decision to accept the unconditional offer of God's forgiveness. In this sense grace is not an extra imported into the moral situation, but is the expression of your actual dependence upon God as the giver of your real existence; and in this sense grace is thoroughly constitutive of the moral situation—a situation which is now recognized to be a relation. And the service which is the consequence of the freeing is likewise thoroughly constitutive of the moral situation, for now service is simply a 'faithful doing' (*fidele facere*), as Luther calls it, that is, a fulfilling in freedom in the world of the work of faith.[2]

---

[1]Romans 7.15.   [2]1 Thessalonians 1.3.

4. Faith as personal

The implications of the liberation of the self in and through forgiveness reach far beyond the individual. For just as the liberating power is one which establishes the reality of the self in terms of relationship, so this same relationship is expressed in free responsibility in the world. Responsibility means freedom as it is given through the forgiveness of God. 'All things are lawful.'[1] This responsible freedom in the world is the clue to the right understanding of man's relation to history and of the development of secularism. To this we shall come in due course.

Meantime, however, I wish to concentrate further on the meaning of faith as historical. In the situation of grace which I have already described as constitutive of the human experience of forgiveness there is implicit a significant further reality. It is that faith is strictly personal. By 'personal' I do not mean merely that it is an individual matter, or that religion, as Whitehead has said, is simply 'what a man does with his solitariness'. Certainly it is only as man stands as a single person before the demand laid upon him that he is aware both of his impotence and of the possibility which is opened up before him. But the commitment of faith, though it necessarily involves solitude, neither begins nor ends in solitariness. It involves solitude before God.

[1] I Corinthians 6.12.

39

The man who is faced with the decision of faith—for or against—'is no longer surrounded by the world . . . he has become an I over against the Thou.'[1] That is to say, he is taken out of the world. He is no longer a part of the world, either in the sense of an all-embracing cosmic order or in the sense of the world of men. Nothing else counts but the summons from God to come to himself. And this means breaking with his old self and entering into a new relationship with God. But simultaneously the dialectic of faith comes into play. For this new relationship with God does not mean the simple negation of the world out of which he is taken. It means the dialectical affirmation of this world. Only now this world is no longer the enclosed and the enclosing entity which it was before the decision of faith. Rather, it is now the place in which personal existence is both expressed and confirmed. It is so strictly the place where faith lives that faith itself may even be called a place and a time.[2] The world itself is now recognized for what it is—the creation of God. That is to say, the man in faith is thrown back into the world which he was ready to leave, to which in truth he had already died: only now this world is no longer his master. But he is its master, it is his world, as the son and heir of God. He therefore takes over responsibility for this world. Its reality is now confirmed as a personal reality. The world is no longer simply an It, but is the place and time of Thou. This possibility of personal being for the world is the meaning of the world as creation. The doctrine of creation does not imply any scientific or ontological status, but simply this possibility

[1] Friedrich Gogarten, *Der Mensch zwischen Welt und Gott*, p. 14.
[2] I owe the phrase 'faith as a place' to Professor William Hamilton, who uses it in an essay, 'The Death of God Theologies Today', in *The Christian Scholar*, March, 1965.

that the world may be fully historical, that is, the place and the time of personal being.

Nevertheless the transience of the world is not abolished. The man of faith lives on as before in the process of decay. This is true not only of his individual life, but also of the life of the societies and structures to which he belongs. He, along with these structures, is moving still towards death. But because he is in faith, he has already broken free from servitude to death. Proleptically he has already been liberated from the sting of death: for he has already entered into the person-to-person relation with God. And the world, which is now his world, is likewise given this possibility of personal relation. That is to say, the world so far as it is henceforth able to share in man's personal and historical existence in relation with God is also given meaning as personal. This is the almost unexplored region of possibility for the world as creation which is hinted at in St Paul's words, 'For the creation waits with eager longing for the revealing of the sons of God . . . because the creation itself will be set free from its bondage to decay and obtain the glorious liberty of the children of God . . .'[1]

Clearly, then, the man of faith is by no means finished with life in this world. This is expressed by St Paul in his clear confession that he has 'not already attained'.[2] But in everything that now comes to him, in every decision which he makes, and in every claim made upon him from the ordinary world, the reality of his sufferings and his actions is lent to him by the prior grace of God's personal relation to him. He does not despair of himself or of the world, and he does not deny the reality of the world and its demands. But the reality of the world is given in its status as creation. The world is given to him. It is no longer an autonomous power which sucks him into itself. It tries to do this, and it

[1]Romans 8.19f.   [2]Philippians 3.12.

can do it. The world is full of slaves who are as helpless as flies caught in a spider's web. This may be true even of those who seem to be the lords of the world. It may be true especially of them. For their pathetic plight is that they have reached positions of power which remain positions of power only when these so-called lords are submissive to the world's power. This is not the power of destiny, but the power of fate. When Ethelbert Stauffer talks about 'the will of history', for example,[1] he is really talking about the impersonal power of fate, viewed as the determinant factor in a world unrelated to God. The man of faith, on the other hand, is ruled not by fate but by destiny. Rather, he shares freely through his personal decision in shaping the world to be the destiny for him and for others which is its historical possibility as creation. So the world is not his master. This holds true in every sphere of life. A man may fall in love and marry either as his fate or as his destiny. As his fate it is nothing more nor less than his yielding to the world as his master. Yet even out of fate the links of destiny may be forged, if a man has courage and decisiveness in face of what Heidegger has called his *Geworfenheit*, his 'thrownness' into the world. For in the strength of the absolute relation to God the personal resolution may free a man from fate and make him truly a creature of destiny.

Destiny is the realm of the personal, but fate is the realm of the impersonal.

It is not easy to be a free person living under destiny, for the bonds of society are very strong. And nations, and smaller societies, including churches, possess immense powers of persuasion towards conformism. Where these powers impel towards the impersonal world of fate, they must be combatted to the utmost. Thus we must be continually ready to ask whether the dogmas we are invited to subscribe

[1]*Christ and the Caesars*, p. 94.

to, whether literally or passively, whether in a church or in a nation, in a political party or even in a small voluntary group, really contain in themselves the possibility of personal being.

In the last resort nothing else counts but the divine reality of personal responsibility in personal freedom. Everything less than this is impersonal, and ends in the bleakness of the collective. Europe—and through Europe the whole world— is in fearful danger of accepting collectivities, whether of race, or ecclesiastical or political dogmas, or of mere opting out of any direct decision at all. And this option, not to decide, is itself an option *against* the reality of personal being. If this option were accepted by all there would be no more history. For history itself is constituted by the personal decisions which arise out of the confrontation in faith of the personal demand of God to each single person.

5. *Faith as a unity in relation*

So far I have spoken of faith as essentially historical, arising as a response to a specific constellation of events and given shape and content by these events. I have distinguished this faith in its historicity from any specific metaphysic, from any mythological form, and from simple moralism. I have spoken of it as a free decision to accept the forgiveness of God in Christ. And lastly I described it as essentially personal, in the sense of an existence in relation with God and with the world as the place where this relation is confirmed and acted out.

In all this I have tacitly set aside the traditional description of faith as being compounded of three elements, *notitia*, *assensus* and *fiducia*, knowledge, assent, and trust. The intention of this threefold division, however, is a sound one: faith does include knowledge, namely, knowledge of certain happenings, and even in a certain sense knowledge of God. And faith does include assent, in the sense of an obedient submission to the claim laid upon you. And lastly, it does include a personal commitment or trust in God. It is therefore an exaggeration to say, for example, as Martin Buber does, that 'you do not need to know something about God in order really to believe in him.'[1] But it is an understandable exaggeration in face of the other extreme, which is so prevalent in the conventional view, that faith is

[1] *Eclipse of God*, p. 40.

44

primarily a subscription to certain statements which are regarded as objectively guaranteed. The New Testament kerygma can certainly not be equated with a series of propositions derived from the apostolic preaching. And not even the Apostles' Creed can be properly regarded as claiming that kind of assent. It is the first words of the Creed which put all its articles into the proper perspective: 'I believe in . . .'

The relation which is indicated by these words between *fides qua creditur*, the faith by which you believe, and *fides quae creditur*, the faith which you believe, cannot be separated in existence. But an existential faith is a unity in relation of the Giver of faith and the believer.

The same consideration determines our view all the way, from the words of Scripture through all creeds and confessions: none may be regarded as absolutely binding, in the sense of being objects somehow elevated above the relativities and the complexities of historical understanding and acceptance. The spectre of the subject-object schema haunts every attempt to speak about the complexities of this situation without falling either into naive subjectivism or equally naive objectivism. It would be also naive of me to claim support from the New Testament, in that it provides no such division into subject and object, since it may rightly be suggested that we are not bound to the thought-forms of the world of the New Testament. And this indeed is our problem: our theological problem is constituted by the historical necessity of speaking in our own language to our own time. This does not, I repeat, necessarily land us in subjectivism, whether of the splendid style of Schleiermacher or of some decadent form of this. But the shabby objectivism of Fundamentalism or near-Fundamentalism, and its variations in sub-Barthian positions, or sub-Calvinist, or the like, is no real solution. It cannot be stated baldly enough that theology is not the repetition of thoughts and words of the Bible or of any of the great theologians of the past.

So the power of faith cannot be reduced to the authoritative demand that you accept a series of pronouncements whose guarantee is in the last resort a man-made guarantee, whether it is the authority of Pope or bible, creed or council. For the true power of faith resides in the gracious act of God in Christ, offering a new start to human existence. The basic objection, therefore, to the traditional threefold formula, with all its variations, is not that it misses the mark entirely, and not that it so easily tips over into an exaggeration of one or other of its elements, but that it tends to petrify in inadequate categories an essentially dynamic situation. It is not able to cope with the offence of the gracious act of God in Christ.

6. Faith as justification

The gracious act of God in Christ: what does this mean? I shall later face the question of what we mean by 'an act of God'. Here we have to ask what it is that Christ brings into the human situation, regarded from the standpoint of faith as something that happens to man. Is it something entirely new, or is it the fulfilment of something already somehow present in human life? Is it the climax of history or its end? Is it what Christ teaches, or is it simply his life, regarded as a manifest revelation of God's character? Or again, is the faith of which we speak the faith which Christ himself holds, and bears witness to in his life, or is this faith which is the *differentia* of Christianity to be understood as faith in Christ?

I propose to take up later what precisely is meant by 'history', in the burning question of the relation of the Jesus of history to the preached Christ. Here I restrict myself to the question of how faith understands itself in relation to the event of Christ. I also leave aside the more general question of how it is possible at all for faith to be related to events of the past. Such questions can only be faced in terms of history as eschatological which we shall deal with later. The claim of faith is undoubtedly that it is so related, and furthermore, that in this relation it comes to its full stature. Faith *is* faith only in and through the revelation of God in Christ.

What is this revelation? It is certainly not enough, and it is even misleading, to say that in the life of Jesus we learn what God is like. For such an interpretation implies a reduction of the life of Jesus to certain characteristic values and essences which means the elimination of the real history of Jesus. This would not matter if it were indeed the case that the addition of certain values and essential ideals to the stock of human information and aspiration (the value of heroic love, say, or of sacrificial service, or the infinite value of the individual, or the lofty teaching of the brotherhood of all men) were able to bring about a radical, or even just a notable, change in our own values and aspirations.

But the truth of our human situation is more complex, and more tragic, than this: it cannot be described merely in terms of certain lacks or defects, which may be made up by a filling up and gradual approximation to the ideal or the norm. This evolutionary moralism is simply not able to cope with the immense abysses of evil and despair in human existence:

> *cliffs of fall*
> *Frightful, sheer, no-man-fathomed.*

What the life of Jesus in its historical reality actually does to us is in the first place to confront us with a judgment upon all that our life consists of. By the 'historical reality' of the life of Jesus I mean something different from the construction of a 'portrait' or biography of that life as it may with more or less (but usually less) unanimity be reconstituted by the aid of literary research. For the present I merely state categorically (what will have to be discussed in more detail later) that the historical Jesus indicates a complex reality which certainly includes some kind of historical 'facts' but is immeasurably more than these (which are indeed abstractions from that complex reality), this

48

immeasurability arising out of the paradoxical and offensive conjunction of the action of God with the human response in faith to that action. The confrontation which is the first stage in the movement of the kerygma or message concerning Jesus, regarded always from the standpoint of the experience of the human subject, is in turn also a highly complex matter, in which the recognition of our incapacity and failure is deepened into the acknowledgment of our sin. In face of the reality of Jesus, and in particular in face of his death upon the cross, as the outcome of what he is, we are invited to see that we simply cannot justify ourselves, nothing that we can do with our lives or ourselves can lead anywhere but to death. There is in the human situation, confronted by the death of Jesus, no hope at all. History, in the common acceptance of the term, is therefore at an end. It has no meaning beyond the ineluctable end of death.

But simultaneously (though in the sequence of thought about it we must call it the second stage) in this human situation there is also an invitation to go further. Besides the judgment on all our life, on its self-assertion, pretensions, and unitary self-justification, we are invited to accept our life anew. This judgment and this invitation come to us as the unified message of the historical reality of the life of Christ. This reality, or this happening, is described in different ways in the New Testament—as a sacrifice,[1] as the coming of a pre-existent divine figure from heaven in the form of a servant who after his death was exalted as Lord,[2] as the inauguration of a new era,[3] and in many other ways. Such descriptions are not mutually exclusive. They all converge upon, and thus are witnesses or pointers to, the reality of the life and death of Jesus as a message of judgment

[1] 1 Corinthians 5.7, Philippians 4.18, Hebrews 9.26.
[2] Philippians 2.6–11. [3] 2 Corinthians 5.17.

49

and of hope for man's life. It is in Christ as the eschatological event that the possibilities for faith are offered. I leave till later a discussion of the highly potentiated term 'eschatology'. Here I content myself by saying that the possibilities offered here may be summarized in the words of St Paul: 'For Christ is the end of the law, that every one who has faith may be justified.'[1]

But these possibilities must not be understood as implying a state of existence. Even though we have here tried to speak in a certain abstraction from the complex historical reality, it *is* an abstraction. The man of faith does not possess justification, or live as justified, in the sense that henceforth he is able to manage his own life as a justified person—even if he adds that of course he is a justified sinner. This is not the case, because if it were it would essentially involve a new law: within the terms of my new self-understanding as justified I can now set out to live and act on my own. The significance of this misunderstanding will become clearer when we come to consider the nature of secularism. This misunderstanding is indeed hard to avoid in terms of traditional theological thinking. For the traditional categories are framed in terms of metaphysical and mythological concepts, such as state and substance; whereas the new possibility in faith is characterized by a new *relation* of man to God and the world. This relation, moreover, is set dynamically in space and time, and must be constantly renewed in decision and in the acceptance of forgiveness.

The most penetrating description of this dynamic relationship is found in St Paul's words about sonship and adoption. In Romans 8.14 *ff* we read:

For all who are led by the Spirit of God are sons of God.
For you did not receive the spirit of slavery to fall back

[1]Romans 10.4.

into fear, but you have received the spirit of sonship. When we cry 'Abba! Father!' it is the Spirit himself bearing witness with our spirit that we are children of God, and if children, then heirs, heirs of God and fellow heirs with Christ, provided we suffer with him in order that we may also be glorified with him.

Again, in Galatians 3.26*ff* we read:

For in Christ Jesus you are all sons of God, through faith . . . And if you are Christ's . . . you are heirs according to the promise. I mean that the heir, as long as he is a child, is no better than a slave, though he is the owner of all the estate; but he is under guardians and trustees until the date set by the father. So with us; when we were children, we were slaves to the elemental spirits of the universe. But when the time had fully come, God sent forth his Son . . . so that we might receive adoption as sons. And because you are sons, God has sent the Spirit of his Son into our hearts, crying 'Abba! Father!' So through God you are no longer a slave but a son, and if a son then an heir.

The immense significance of this description of the possibilities offered to faith will occupy us especially when we look at the relation of the man of faith to the world. Here we have simply to note that in faith we are accepted by God as having come of age, and are invited to enter upon our inheritance, which is the world viewed henceforth not as cosmic fate but as historical possibility.

This symbol of man's acceptance by God, man's 'coming of age' or 'maturity', is the subject of a great deal of discussion today, especially in connexion with Dietrich Bonhoeffer's use of the term (*Mündigkeit*). In spite of the confusions and extravagances which have attached to the discussion, the concept is certainly more potent in our time as a means of understanding what I term 'historical possibility' than the traditional term 'justification'. But the old term and the new point to the same reality, namely, God's acceptance of man. The consequent dialectic which is inherent in this 'maturity' or 'adulthood' of man will be discussed when we analyse the nature of Christian secularity.

7. *Faith not an empirical phenomenon*

In all that has so far been said about the nature of Christian faith one serious question has been implicit throughout, to which we must now address ourselves. A full answer, however, will only be possible when we have examined the implications of an eschatological faith in its relation to ongoing society.[1] The question is whether faith is an observable empirical phenomenon.

The ordinary man—or let us try to define that elusive figure more precisely and say the theologically uninstructed person who is interested in Christianity either as an observer or as one who would like, if he only knew how, to be more closely involved—is likely to link his question about the results of faith with the cynical or the pessimistic suspicion that highfalutin theological investigations are eminently capable of constructing a model of faith which is merely 'academic'. That is, he will wonder whether theologizing makes any difference to living. And he is suspicious of assertions which bear no observable or demonstrable connexion with actual phenomena.

His suspicion is perfectly proper, so far as the alleged convictions of faith are not in some way fulfilled in their strict relation to persons and society. Reinhold Niebuhr once spoke somewhere with scathing accuracy of the theolo-

[1] See pp. 199 *ff*. below.

53

gical students who, when they were faced with an intractable problem, straightway 'took an elevator for the eternal'. And behind the attitude which provoked this remark there lies the devastating challenge of Kierkegaard to conventional Christianity, or 'Christendom', as he called it, in distinction from 'New Testament Christianity'.[1] In his last years Kierkegaard was particularly critical of the disparity between the assertions of Christendom about faith, and the actual empirical consequences of that faith. For him the whole reliance of the Danish Lutheran tradition upon 'faith alone' was merely a hypocritical excuse for simple and direct enjoyment of life. Faith had become entirely invisible.

We must give our whole-hearted agreement to Kierkegaard, so far as his criticism was directed against an uncommitted faith, a faith which indeed is no faith, but unbelief, a decision, in fact, against the reality of the relation of judgment and forgiveness from God.

But does this then mean that faith must be entirely observable and demonstrable, as a phenomenon in the world? I do not think so.

This is a difficult thing for the ordinary man, with his unreflecting trust in the empirical world, to swallow. He is quick to see the absurdity of a faith which is so invisible that it makes no difference, is not distinctive, but is simply conformed in every respect (save that of words and an occasional appearance at a service of public worship) to the ordinary world. But he is also slow to see that the very dialectic of faith which he dimly recognizes by his criticism is of such a kind that he just cannot have everything clear and simple. A man of faith, he thinks, should be simply a man whose life is visibly fruitful with the works of faith. But what does he really mean by this? When the Nazis in

[1] Cf. my edition of *The Last Years*, Kierkegaard's journals 1853-55, London, 1965.

Hitler Germany were in process of destroying those conspirators of whom Graf Moltke is the noble exemplar, the President of the People's Court said, 'These people should worry about the other world, and leave us here in peace.'[1] That particular ordinary man, the Nazi President Freisler, did not believe in the 'other world'. Likewise the ordinary man of today does not believe in that 'other world' as imaged in the traditional forms and formulas. But as a rule he does not reach that extreme of hatred of the man of faith which would prompt him to speak like that Nazi judge. On the contrary, he longs to find images and forms which would furnish visible confirmation of the claims of faith. And the only images and forms left to him are empirical 'fruits'.

So far as he is truly asking for the reality of faith to be expressed in the fruits of love, surely he is right in his longing. But the problem we are facing is precisely the nature of these fruits. And if what is looked for is simply directly observable phenomena, such as could not be gainsaid by anyone, because they are as manifest as the sun or the moon, then it must be just as simply said that this is not how things are. This expectation is really for a series of miracles, in the sense of objectifiable wondrous happenings, whose origin is the direct effect of faith, and whose consequence in turn is supposed to be the empirical establishment of the truth of faith. Basically, this is the desire for a mythological and undialectical substitute for faith and its works.

But the manifestation of faith is not simple, but dialectical. In Professor Bultmann's words, 'the grace of God is not visible like worldly entities. His treasures are hidden in earthly vessels [2 Corinthians 4.7]. The resurrection life is manifested in the world in the guise of death [2 Corinthians 12.9]. Only in human weakness is the power of God made

[1]Moltke, *Letzte Briefe*, p. 37.

known.'[1] It is when this question of the manifestation of faith is asked that the existence of the man of faith is recognized as thoroughly paradoxical. The paradox is the reflection of the supreme paradox of forgiveness. It is impossible to reduce the manifestation of faith to a formula like 'being for others', for this is an attempt to get rid of the essential ambiguity. Even Christ's self-giving remains ambiguous, for at no point does his life impose truth upon others. This is the crux of the paradoxical nature of the end of all human life in Christ, the eschatological reality of Christ as the Word made flesh. To the pervasive significance of this eschatological existence we must return, when we look at the meaning of history and of God's act in history.[2] In the meantime we have to recognize the depth of Luther's formula, *simul iustus simul peccator*. Both faith and its works are determined by the reality of the forgiveness of the man who yet remains a sinner. So these concepts are strictly theological, not phenomenological. That is to say, we are not entitled, when we ask about the manifestation of faith, to look for a simple, directly observable, state of being or state of affairs. Consequently we cannot make a catalogue of the possible manifestations of faith, by means of which we may judge the reality of faith. When St Paul makes what looks like a catalogue of the 'fruits of the Spirit' (in Galatians 5.22), he is not providing material for an unambiguous inference concerning the truth of faith, but rather indicating the reality of being for others as constitutive of the work of faith. But the manifestation of this being for others cannot be removed from the ambiguous realm in which the reality of faith consists in the perpetual tension of the relation with God. Here is where faith is

[1]Rudolf Bultmann, *Primitive Christianity*, Fontana ed., London, 1956, p. 231.
[2]See below pp. 117-31.

primarily active—in this tension in which it is renewed, against all appearances, in the midst of the tribulations and temptations which are integral to life, and in the face also of the doubt which is the permanent other side of the possibility of faith—as a provisional, makeshift, uncertain and fighting certainty.

When this is seen as the primary and central activity of faith, that is, when faith is seen as concerned primarily with the relation with God, then it cannot be primarily a matter of phenomenology. Nor can it be primarily a matter of the decision of the man of faith. What is primary here is the initiating grace of God, who has not only initiated but also continues and sustains this relation. Certainly, from the standpoint of the man of faith the issue of faith is love in hope. But from the standpoint of the grace of God which constitutes this faith and makes it possible, the conclusion cannot be other than in the same grace which is his being towards man. The traditional form for expressing this conclusion is that of sight or vision, the *visio beatifica* as the outcome and end of faith.

Certainly this is a dusty answer for the ordinary man, and it leaves unanswered many questions about the relation of faith to history. We shall have to look again at this whole matter in the context of the meaning of secularism.

Meantime, we must provisionally conclude that the answer to the ordinary man about the manifest *differentia* of faith cannot make use of any phenomenological evidence to demonstrate anything for or against the reality of faith. You cannot prove faith by its fruit. Nor can you disprove it. Faith remains in its own peculiar realm, ambiguous, unpredictable, in constant tension both with God and with the world. Faith remains true to itself: it is neither sight nor proof.

This is true not only of the individual's faith, but also of the expressions or deposits of faith as they may be found in the course of the history of Christendom. No exercise is more ambiguous than the attempt to prove the truth of faith by demonstrating its benefits to the world. Strictly speaking, there is no over-all meaning to be discerned in history, and this is true equally of the so-called ordinary events of history and of the so-called redemptive history or *Heilsgeschichte*. But if faith cannot be demonstrated, neither can it be disproved. Faith remains faith, and by its mere existence it involves a total response.

8. Faith and the traditional arguments for God's existence

One important corollary of the eminent historicity of faith is that the traditional ways of 'proving' God's existence are not adequate as independent proofs. They are not adequate because they do not take account of the way in which faith takes its rise and its form. This is true, at least, of the cosmological, the teleological and the moral argument for the existence of God. That is to say, each of these arguments is able to reach the conclusion 'God exists' only because they contain the hidden presupposition that God exists. But the actual course of the arguments logically excludes this presupposition. Each of the arguments demands a leap from the conditioned to the unconditioned which the discursive reason is by its nature unable to take. Whether you begin from the contingency of all things in the cosmos, or from the evidences of design in nature, or from the sovereignty of the moral will, you are brought up short against the limits of rational enquiry: if you begin from this world you cannot go beyond it. Thus the logical consequence of an enquiry into the nature of the cosmos, or of the moral demand, is pantheism, or humanism, or nihilism. Either you conclude that God is the cosmos, or that the cosmos is a self-contained entity in which cause and effect, or design, or the assertion of the moral imperative, have meaning only in themselves, and that any step beyond this self-enclosed entity is impossible.

Then what of the so-called ontological argument for the existence of God? Here is certainly something different. The argument could only be formulated on the basis of that 'infinite qualitative difference' between God and man, which was so axiomatic for Kierkegaard, but which is by no means absent from earlier scholastic thought. It was Anselm of Canterbury who may be said to have invented the ontological argument, though there is at least an anticipation of it in Augustine.[1] It was on the basis of his faith that Anselm tried to clarify the concept of God in the following words: 'We believe that Thou art something than which nothing greater can be conceived.' As Erich Frank has justly said, while this definition accounts for the majesty of God, 'it constitutes a simply unsurmountable difficulty for human reason . . . how can we be sure of the existence of a Being which transcends every thing we know, even our own capacity of thought? Can he who says there is no such God except in our imagination ever be disproved?'[2]

Nevertheless, the reality of God, which Anselm here attempts to understand, and which in fact he seems able to understand only in the paradoxical sense of yielding his understanding, is not simply beyond the reach of man. This reality is beyond the reach of man so far as that reach is taken to be exhaustively defined in terms of man's capacity for discursive thought. In these terms once again, as with the other arguments, we cannot get beyond the conditioned world (in this case the world which is conditioned by our own thought about it, even if our thought about it should raise the possibility of the unconditioned). In fact, all

[1] See *de libero arbitrio* II, 6.14.
[2] *Philosophical Understanding and Religious Truth*, New York, 1955, p. 34*f.*

four arguments may now be described as just variations of one argument: the attempt to move from the conditioned to the unconditioned. And as an argument it collapses, brought up short against the limits of rational enquiry.

But if the reality of God is thus beyond the reach of the understanding, it is not beyond the faith which Anselm already held, in however inchoate a form. This faith, for Anselm too, is eminently historical. That is, it is not possible apart from Christ. Thus if Anselm's argument is taken (as he tried to take it, in the letter though not in the spirit of the *Proslogion*) as a movement of thought towards transcendent being, it fails. But if it is taken as it can be, and, I suggest, must be, within the realm of historical existence which is postulated by his faith in God through Christ, then he is in a very different position. The power of his argument then moves within, and never leaves, the realm of historical existence. His very attempt to think God as real is then to be seen as an attempt to grasp transcendence on the basis of that very transcendence which has already entered his life in the historical faith. Anselm, that is to say, is not just thinking in a void. Neither here nor in his other great argument in the *Cur Deus Homo?* is he really arguing *Christo remoto*. But he is thinking in terms of the faith he has already accepted. And this faith remains, despite all his ratiocination—indeed, as confirming the limits of that rational enquiry—a risk: it demands a *salto mortale*, which engages the whole person.

The intellectual statement of the ontological argument is a reflection of the relation between the transcendent God and the man of faith in its historical form. If you believe in the transcendent God as present in Christ in history, and in your personal history, then the ontological assertion is bound to follow. We must certainly agree with Locke in his remarks about Descartes' formulation of the argument, which hold good also for Anselm's formulation, that 'it is an ill way of establishing this truth and silencing atheists, to lay the whole stress of so important a point as this upon that sole foundation.'[1] No more than the older traditional proofs, which depend upon this one, can the ontological argument be held to be an independent proof of the existence of God. But in the context of a historical faith the ontological argument has a necessary, if subsidiary, place. The importance of this conclusion will become clear when we look at some modern theological short-cuts in the discussion about the possibility of God-language.[2]

The reality of faith, then, is not dependent upon the stringency of the traditional arguments for God's existence. It may, however, be strengthened by specific uses of these arguments—not as self-contained arguments, but rather as dependent on the historical situation of faith, and deriving their strength from the insight of faith into the paradoxical reality of the Word become flesh. And on the other hand, these arguments in themselves, when their intrinsic effeteness is exposed, by no means carry with them, when they are demolished as logical structures, the collapse of the much more subtle construction of faith.

But it would be a misunderstanding to conclude from this that the reality of faith is an entirely subjective matter, indifferent to the patient failures of the reason. We intend to show that the historicity of faith works by categories which surpass, though they include, the means appropriate to the discursive reason. This does not mean that faith takes refuge in some form of directness or immediacy. The mystical or pseudo-mystical reliance upon some kind of

[1] *Concerning Human Understanding*, IV, 10.7, Fontana ed., London, 1964, p. 381.
[2] See pp. 186ff. below.

ineffable experience is a peripheral matter, which we mention only because the traditional philosophical reserve at this point so often is ready to make this minor concession —as though faith could be reduced to a matter of private experience, or eccentric or esoteric taste. Directness, or the claim to a mystical vision, on the basis of a divine 'spark' implanted in the soul, is, as Kierkegaard said bluntly, paganism. Quite strictly, this means that neither in the human soul nor in the powers and beings in the world may one speak of the immediate presence of God. This is not to deny that in some way we may nevertheless speak of the presence of God in the soul and in the powers and beings and events of the world. But we may never properly identify faith with a sense or perception or sight of God. Faith is a relation which takes its rise in the otherness of God. God is simply not present in the sense of direct and unmediated being in the world: so he can neither be 'sensed' in it, nor derived from it. Equally, he cannot be found in the human soul as an immediately given element. He is not an element in the world. When St Paul speaks of the 'beggarly elements'[1] he means those powers and beings in the world which are beggarly precisely because in faith they have been deprived of their powerful claims to be divine. In faith the world has been de-divinized. It is henceforth simply itself, and that means that to faith the world is waiting to be accepted once more for what it is, namely, the creation of God. But between the Creator and the creature there is a gulf, which is the very reason why the encounter of faith—not the 'sense of the presence', or the 'perception' of the divine, or the 'feeling' or even the intuition of God—is possible at all.

By way of indirect inference, then, God cannot be reached. By way of direct feeling he is equally inaccessible.

[1] Galatians 4.9.

Only by way of faith, in response to what God does in history, can he be encountered, and either affirmed or denied.

We must therefore now turn to a closer examination of what we mean by history.

II. HISTORY

1. Introduction

In the course of the story of Christianity many different concepts have at different times achieved pre-eminence as the dominant clue for understanding what Christianity is essentially concerned with. Justification, predestination, evolutionary idealism, the Word of God: in a manner which is capable of explanation at many different levels, sociological and theological, but is never wholly understandable, these and other concepts have in turn become almost axiomatic as the way of expressing the driving Christian concern.

It lies beyond the scope of these reflections to attempt an analysis of any, far less of all, of these concepts. The lesson which we draw, however, from the story of their rise and fall is one of reserve, even of a necessary scepticism, regarding the absolute claim which each in turn has made. Is it not possible that the adventure of Christian faith is greater than all the explanations of it which have hitherto prevailed? And that we do not lie at the end of a brief episode in Western history, but rather stand before unimagined and unimaginable prospects, in the power of faith?

In our time the concept of history has begun to claim so much attention that it is on the way to reaching the predominant position in theology. It has already been elevated by one theologian to the status of a doctrine.[1]

[1] By John McIntyre, in his book *The Christian Doctrine of History*, London, 1957.

In the presuppositions of our time it has already become so significant that the worst thing that can be said of a theologian with whom you disagree (worse than denying him a sense of humour) is that he has embarked on a 'flight from history'. One of the purposes of what follows is to rescue the concept of history from the region of unexamined presuppositions, where diatribe flourishes, and to make a reasoned critical advance possible.

It is clear that for Christian theology the concern with history is inextricably connected with the central realities of its subject matter: I mean above all the reality of the life of Christ. Without pre-determining the way in which that life is to be understood, circumscribed, and defined, we may make a start by saying that theology has to do with a message concerning Christ which is not separable from Christ's historical existence. It is this at first sight quite simple view which has in our time intensified the concern with Christianity as 'historical'.

But of course this concern is not new, any more than it is arbitrary. The assertion at the beginning of the Fourth Gospel that 'the Word was made flesh, and dwelt among us' is clearly reflected in the modern transliteration which asserts that Christian faith has to do pre-eminently with history. And no matter how ambiguous this word 'history' is, and whatever the qualifications we shall have to add, the following provisional definition of history, from the Christian standpoint, cannot be negated without our negating the very ground of Christian faith: that history, namely, is the term by which we seek to understand the reality of God's relation to man. It is the term which includes both the reality of man in time and space, in his unique, datable and localizable particularity, and God in his gracious condescension towards man. In the context of this affirmation 'history' is indeed more than a term: it is the all-inclusive framework—more, it is the very reality in which God and man come together, and come together, moreover, in such a way that man's very existence may henceforth be summarily described as historical, and God's existence, too, may only be apprehended as historical.

It may well be asked why, if this emphasis upon history is so all-important for Christian faith, it should only be in our time that it has become so pressing. The answer to this question cannot be simple. In one sense it lies in the mere lethargy of men, as they seek an answer to the question of the reason for their existence, and for the existence of an ongoing structure into which they find themselves thrown when they enter into life. In a deeper sense the answer lies in the very necessities of that ongoing structure. The questions, for instance, which St Paul or the author of the Fourth Gospel necessarily faced, as they had to struggle with the problems of the new faith in its relation both to the old Israel and to the Hellenistic world, were different questions from those which, say, St Augustine had to face when Alaric of the Goths sacked the eternal city, Rome, in the year 410 A.D. And so throughout the generations the questions and the answers have been appropriate to their situation.

But there is, in spite of the inevitable relativities and thus the shifting ground of interest and the taking up and the discarding of ever new conceptual tools, an important sense in which the emphasis on history has been from the beginning, and is bound to remain, the crux of theology. Thus the hermeneutical tools by which we handle the Christian message and seek to interpret it are themselves the product of a slow historical self-understanding. And it is hard to envisage any hermeneutical advance which would entirely ignore or discount this whole emphasis upon history.

It was, however, only in the eighteenth century that the

typically modern historical interest arose. Only with the rise in that rationalist age of an enquiring spirit concerning the legitimacy of Christian faith did the biblical documents begin to undergo a more rigorous scrutiny, a scrutiny which has continued with increasing subtlety and persistence into our own time. In this spirit the dominant question was how the biblical foundations of Christian faith were to be regarded. Lessing, the great spirit of the *Aufklärung* in Germany, answered this question with deceptive simplicity: you must read your bible in the same way as you read Livy. In other words, the question of the relation of Christian faith to the past could not be settled by any authoritative pronouncement, whether of church councils or of the Pope as representative of the sanctity and inviolability of the Christian tradition. Men, moreover, were tired of religious wars such as had devastated Europe during the seventeenth century, and were ready to ask whether their problems, and their differences, could not be approached under the common sign of reason. Thus it was that the bible, as the acknowledged documentary foundation of Christianity, came to be submitted to the earnest scrutiny of scholars of a new kind. They wanted to ask questions about the authenticity, and hence the reliability, of the bible precisely as a *historical* document. Out of these beginnings there arose the splendid structure of biblical criticism, which has since that time acquired many different parts, philology, archaeology, comparative religion, form-criticism, and so on.[1]

It was this emergence of biblical criticism as an autonomous enquiry, submissive to no rules or authorities outside those proper to its own aim, which made it possible for the enquiry concerning history as such, in terms, that is, of the historicity of Christianity, to become in due course the

[1]A splendid study and source book for the rise of biblical criticism is Werner Kümmel's *Das Neue Testament*, 1958.

dominant conception for the realization of the true authority in Christian faith. This authority has come to be recognized, no longer as a heteronomous demand laid upon men from a powerful worldly authority, no longer as an alien force: but as the very reality of history itself, as theonomous, as the place where God was present, and is present. It is in virtue of the recognition of this mysterious and paradoxical authority that we are able to speak of the reality of history as the clue to our understanding of man's existence.

In brief, out of a dispassionate enquiry into the legitimacy and credibility of the documentary sources, the point has now been reached where we are able to ask just what it implies that we should repeat, with the Fourth Gospel, that the Word became flesh, just what it means that in the ongoing course of history we should still be confronted with the question of Jesus, 'Who do *you* say that I am?'[1] Christian faith is thus thrown back upon its own historicity. And in answering properly the question of its own sources, it is now able to offer a view of history which can be paradigmatic for the whole of human existence.

It should be noted that I am speaking of the rise into full consciousness of what is truly a *theological* question about history. That the answer adumbrated by Lessing, and followed up so assiduously in biblical criticism to our own time, does not follow the traditional theological lines, is in itself an indication of the revolution in our understanding of Christian history. It is of course true that alongside this interest in the historicity of the biblical records there has developed an interest in man's history in general. It was Voltaire, according to R. G. Collingwood, who 'invented' the name 'philosophy of history'[2]; and one might add that there also arose about the same time other specific interests in man's past, in his remote past, as evi-

[1]Mark 8.29.   [2] *The Idea of History*, London, 1946, p. 1.

denced in the rise of the new science of archaeology, and in other civilizations, as well as in the connexions between those past happenings and man's contemporary social, economic and political structures. In other words, there was a wide-ranging critical and creative interest in all of the past that had some bearing upon man's present life. And in very general terms one must note that the framework in which these interests were developed was one which implied the continuity of man's history and the forms of his social life with those of his past. This framework of continuous life was especially the insight of the Romantic movement.

Nevertheless, it is the theological question as I have outlined it which has provided the impetus for a modern reassessment of the matter of history. The intense self-consciousness which Christian faith in its authentic restlessness has always engendered has in our time touched this question of history in a new way.

As we have already noted, the question has not been simply neglected or ignored till modern times. It is somewhat more than just implicit in the claim of the gospel that in the man Jesus, God is to be encountered. Thus we read in John 6.41ff.:

The Jews then murmured at him, because he said, 'I am the bread which came down from heaven.' They said, 'Is not this Jesus, the son of Joseph, whose father and mother we know? How does he now say, "I have come down from heaven"?'

And it was after this that many of the disciples of Jesus, who found what he said 'a hard saying', drew back and no longer went about with him.[1]

The disciples drew back because they could not swallow the claim that the Jesus they knew, the man from Nazareth, the datable and localizable individual man, was sent by

[1]John 6.66.

God with such an authority that every one 'who sees the Son and believes in him should have eternal life'.[1] It is this claim which, as I say, points to the historicity in the very heart of Christian faith. And in a more obvious way St Paul was struggling with the mystery of the historical call of the old Israel and the mystery of the rejection of Christ by Israel, and was thus concerned, in the categories which he partly inherited, and partly forged for himself, with what we should now describe as the meaning of the historicity of the gospel.

But the relativities of the situation in which these New Testament writers found themselves did not permit the clear emergence of the category of history. An explicit realization of this category came only with St Augustine. But he too did not understand the category of history in terms which permitted a fully historical formulation. He was certainly vividly aware of the unrepeatability and irreversibility of history. But his thought was dominated by the conception of an immense teleological process. Erich Frank has made this positive contribution of Augustine to the conception of history very clear.[2] And we may certainly recognize the great debt which all subsequent understanding of Christian faith owes to him. In the complex structure of his thought the figure of Christ is central, as unique and determinative, whose life once upon a time is also once for all. Augustine's concrete starting-point was his concern to find meaning in history from the standpoint of the break-up of Roman civilization. He had the specific apologetic intention of proving to the Romans that the collapse of the empire was not due to Christian neglect of the worship of the gods, but on the contrary to their own vices. As he

[1]John 6.40.
[2]In his essay 'The role of history in Christian thought' in *Wissen, Wollen, Glauben.*

developed his argument, however, he produced a vision of the heavenly kingdom, in conflict with earthly kingdoms, and moving towards its own glorious triumph.

Augustine's grand achievement was to state the reality of Christ's historicity in such a way that due account was taken, for the first time, both of the individual's position and of the whole structure of human society in relation to God's historical design. Transience, sheer transience, was thus overcome in his thought; but not by being abolished. Time was not dealt with by being emptied of meaning; on the contrary, time and temporality were given immense significance in virtue of his faith in the coming of Christ 'in the fulness of the times'. In spite of the fearful questionings and the terrible sufferings of men, as Augustine was so well aware of them and so well able to depict them, the essential melancholy of the old view, and indeed of all pre-christian views, of man's life was now abolished. The melancholy which we may all feel when we permit our fantasy to roam unchecked over the countless generations of men, both gone and still to come, over the devouring and insatiable powers of oblivion, able to swallow up so much that once seemed to be fixed and secure for ever in men's memories, over the apparently senseless rise and fall of individuals and of civilizations—this melancholy, which was summed up so poignantly long ago by the Anglo-Saxon poet, when he wrote of man's soul being like a bird which flits for a moment into the warm and lighted hall, out of the darkness, then flies out again into the darkness—this melancholy has been replaced in the Augustinian view of history by an intense realism which is the reflection of a passionate Christian faith.

But not even Augustine's formulation of his faith was able to provide permanent categories. Certainly, they were carried over into the middle ages, and provided a framework for the whole of mediaeval society. But in his basic conception of a goal to which all history was moving, Augustine was unable to avoid the image of a goal lying at the end of history, in apocalyptic and mythological formulations which have proved inadequate to the very historicity they seek to express. For no teleological conception of history is able to contain the paradoxical reality of Christ. A typical conventional formulation in modern times of Augustine's view may be found in the present Dean of York's analysis. Thus we read that for Augustine 'history is the recruiting-ground where men and women out of every race and class and language are enrolled, one by one, as members of the Heavenly City.'[1] It is indeed true that one of the peculiar merits of Augustine's view of history is that each individual Christian is recognized, in virtue of his faith, as being caught up into the eschatological reality of Christ in such a way that time and the world are overcome. But this individualism, which is again rightly understood in the context of the heavenly city, can no longer be so naively envisaged as citizenship of the heavenly city. For this context of the heavenly city has collapsed: its teleological impetus no longer holds the imagination or the conviction of the individual Christian. The place offered by Augustine for the Christian to be at home is no longer there. So there is a naive short-circuit in the Dean's analysis when he concludes that 'for those who share Augustine's faith, history still derives its meaning . . . from the fact that it is the sphere in which the love of God for every individual soul is ceaselessly exercised for man's salvation, until his new creation, the Heavenly City, is complete.'[2] The naivety lies not in the fact that we do not share Augustine's faith, but that we cannot share his reasons. His reasons for under-

[1]Alan Richardson, *History Sacred and Profane*, London, 1964, p. 62.
[2]*ibid.*, p. 63.

75

standing history as he did, and his ability to express his reasons in the teleological imagery which he used, no longer hold for us. The chief reason why they no longer hold for us is that history is both more inclusive, and less able to offer a simple resting-place, so to speak at its end, when, as the Dean says, the heavenly city 'is complete'. History is more inclusive, in the sense that we can no longer regard it simply as a 'sphere' in which God exercises his love. Rather, the modern insight (as we shall see in more detail later) is that history is that by and in which we believe that God comes to man. So history is also less able to offer a simple resting-place because, being all that we know, knowing nothing beyond it, it is at the same time a place in which man, though he has nowhere else, cannot be simply at home. The Dean wishes to solve this crucial tension of human existence, and its concurrent paradox for the mind, by a straightforward and direct pietist conception of individual salvation. The evolutionary theories of liberal theology are not far below the surface of this view. Augustine, incomparably more subtle, combines his individual faith with a reasonable hope, together with a reasonable scepticism, concerning civilization.

We cannot accept Augustine's formulations. Far less then can we accept a modern liberal view which has reduced the heavenly city to a progressive movement which thus gives meaning to history. Our critique of Augustine must rest upon a critique of the very concept of a teleological process, viewed as an immense drama of *Heilsgeschichte*, or story of redemption. For our contention in what follows will be that it is not by any such dramatization of the historical 'process', but by a re-thinking of the eschatological reality of Christ, that a new style of living may be made possible through Christian faith. It may well be that no images at all can be utilized out of the traditional store.

For the old images of the end reel before the dizzy immensities both of the world without and the world within. So Christian faith, in its very historicity, no longer permits us to discern in any direct fashion the existence of a 'purpose' in history. Far less may we derive from such a general hypothesis of a purpose in course of being achieved and completed any details of its fulfilment (such as the punishment or destruction of evil and the advancement or reward of good). With these denials we are of course also denying the secularized version of Augustine's teleological view, which regards progress as inevitable.

That intense personal union in Augustine's own life of faith and reason, of his Christian conviction and his trust in the methods of Greek philosophy, broke down long ago, when the *corpus christianum* of the middle ages was fragmented in the Renaissance. So we are forced to ask all over again, for ourselves in our own historical situation, as heirs both of Augustine and of the Renaissance, what we make of our human existence.

2. *History as the presentness of the past*

Christian faith, I said, has been thrown back on its own historicity. This means essentially that through the critical study of the biblical records it has been forced to ask in particular, and with novel force, the question concerning the historicity of Jesus. This question in its earlier phase, during the age of so-called liberal theology, took the form of a polemical effort to separate the 'Jesus of history' from the 'Christ of dogma'. A sustained investigation of the sources would be able—such was the hope—to reconstruct the biography of Jesus in such a way that we could thenceforth dispense with the dogmatic 'accretions'. In this way we should reach the simple 'facts'.

But, as Albert Schweitzer concludes in his monumental study of the nineteenth century efforts to construct such a life of Jesus, 'There is nothing more negative than the result of the critical study of the life of Jesus . . . We must be prepared to find that the historical knowledge of the personality and life of Jesus will not be a help, but perhaps even an offence to religion . . .'[1]

These words are the epitaph on the liberal attempt to get behind the dogmatic picture of Christ to the simple Jesus of history. This attempt did indeed result in something that might be called an offence to religion. It is not, how-

[1] *The Quest of the Historical Jesus*, London, 1922, pp. 396, 399.

ever, an offence in the strict New Testament sense of the *skandalon* of the Word become flesh, which cannot be eliminated without the elimination of Christianity. But it is an offence in the sense that it refuses to face the ambiguity which is present in a thoroughgoing historical understanding. Instead, this liberal view produced a diminished figure, a fictitious figure, indeed, a nineteenth-century Jesus who was a reflection of the writer's own image. This Jesus could be seen variously as a hero of faith, or as the wisest of teachers, or even as a model for direct imitation. He could be seen in a bewildering variety of roles, as the instigator of progress, in which the kingdom of God which he proclaimed was regarded as identical with the ongoing sweep of modern civilization, as the great socialist and pacifist, and again as the poet of a life of inwardness and individual devotion.

All these forms, and others besides, may be seen in the succession of biographies and portraits which have appeared over the generations immediately preceding us. All of them are misguided. They are controlled by a single fatal assumption, namely, that there is open to us, as we stand at our particular point in space and time, the possibility of an immediate relationship with events and persons of the past. It is what I should term the fallacy of immediacy, the notion that by means of a scientific, critical investigation you may be connected with a figure of the past, in this case with the figure of Jesus of Nazareth, in unambiguous immediacy. The assumption is that you are able to stand outside history, and as a neutral observer get into contact with the 'facts', the 'objective facts', of the past.

It is not my intention to go over the whole story of this phase in detail. Nor indeed do I wish to attempt any detailed contribution to the phase in which we now find ourselves. It would demand a book in itself to resume with any fairness

79

the extraordinary wealth and variety of contributions to the discussion. I wish rather to make some general observations which have, I hope, a bearing upon the particular investigation into what we mean by historicity.

First, I should say that it is clear, from the débâcle suffered by the liberal critical investigation, that the time of the historical approach to the life of Jesus is past. It has proved to be a cul-de-sac. There is no way of reaching a picture of the facts which is objective in the sense of being unassailable, unproblematic, and generally accepted. And even if there were, *per impossibile*, such a general agreement, it would not be satisfactory. For the facts would have to include much more than has been regarded, on this approach, as the factual source of Christian faith, if justice is to be done to that faith itself.

But this does not mean that the work of historical investigation is worthless or senseless. On the contrary, this investigation is thoroughly competent within its own sphere to assess the probability of certain facts which are available to it by its own particular methods. And it can go a certain distance with some confidence along the way of uncovering (in Ranke's phrase) *'wie es eigentlich gewesen'*, how things really were in the past. The signal illustration in our time of what scientific literary investigation of the sources can produce is to be found in Bultmann's early study of Jesus, published in English as *Jesus and the Word*. The results which Bultmann presents there are all the more significant because they are achieved on the basis of the most delicate and precise investigation. Bultmann claims that it is possible to establish 'a consistent picture' of the message of Jesus.[1] Furthermore, he reaches the conclusion that ' no sane person can doubt that Jesus stands as the founder behind the historical movement whose first distinct stage is

[1] *Jesus and the Word*, London, 1960, p. 17.

represented by the oldest Palestinian community.'[1] (It is incidentally noteworthy that Bultmann has consistently maintained that there are 'simple facts of deeds and events' which can be established 'as they really were' in the sense that the objectifying look can attempt to know them[2]: not that they may be simply and directly apprehended as the substitute for man's dialectical relation to history. I note these points in order to help to remove the unscholarly and boring reiteration that Bultmann is not interested in history, or is a mere subjectivist, and so on.)

All the same, this is a very different and much more modest claim than the positivist assumption that by means of this kind of historical investigation we may attain to an unambiguous connexion with a particular figure of the past. As Martin Kähler saw clearly long ago, 'historical facts which scientific investigation has first to clarify cannot as such become experiences of faith.'[3] But Kähler goes on to say something that cannot, it seems to me, be so easily accepted. 'Thus the history of Jesus and Christian faith flow apart like oil and water, they are like oil and water in that they do not mix, as soon as the magic of enthusiastic portrayal has lost its power.'[4] It is true that all historical investigation is only capable of yielding approximate results, nothing more than probabilities which may be accepted with varying degrees of confidence. Of absolute results—and thus of the positing of an absolute and unambiguous relationship with the construction reached by such results—there can be

---

[1]*ibid.*, p. 17.

[2]Rudolf Bultmann, '*Zum Problem der Entmythologisierung*', in *Kerygma und Mythos* VI, pp. 20–27. The relevant sentence is: '*So wenig dieser [der objektivierende Blick] den geschichtlichen Sinn einer Tat, eines Ereignisses erfasst, so sehr kann und muss er doch die einfachen Fakten der Taten und Ereignisse zu erkennen suchen und in diesem Sinne feststellen, "wie es gewesen ist".*'

[3]*Der sogennante historische Jesus und der geschichtliche biblische Christus*, p. 74.

[4]*ibid.*

81

no question. Far less can there be any question of our
finding in this kind of investigation a demonstrable ground
for our faith.

But does this necessary reserve, even scepticism, concerning the accessibility of assured historical results, mean that
we are simply to abandon the investigation? Does it mean
that there is no significant connexion between the historical
material and the position of the investigator? Does it
mean, for example, that Bultmann's life-work of study of
the sources is a mere diversion, whose only result is that
there are no results? Are the history of Jesus and Christian
faith simply like oil and water?

At this point the ambiguity in the word 'history' begins
to become oppressive. History can mean man's past, but
it can also mean 'the knowledge which men strive to build
up about their past.'[1] In modern German this ambiguity
has been to some extent avoided, or at least brought out
into the open, by the development of two different words:
Historie to describe the enquiry into the past and the material
results obtained by such scientific historical investigation,
and *Geschichte* to describe man's past, what has happened.
Before we ask further what this admittedly unclear definition
of *Geschichte* really implies, it is possible at least to see already
that there are two distinct elements in the concept of
history, and to the extent that this is so we may welcome the
German distinction as useful.[2] However, the separation of

[1]Raymond Aron, art. 'Philosophy of History' in Chambers' *Encyclo-
paedia*, vol. 7, p. 147.
[2]It is possible to make the distinction in a somewhat different way,
namely, between *Historie* as what really happened and *Geschichte* as
'significant' happening. *Historie* is then the term appropriate for a
positivist view, and *Geschichte* that for an idealist view. However, it is
questionable whether one may ever speak of attaining to what really
happened except in terms of a probable reconstruction. And to rescue

the two elements can easily be misleading, if it is then supposed that they are to be found separated in actuality. For they are always found in conjunction, indeed, inseparably united. As Aron says, 'Reality and knowledge of reality are inseparable, in a way that has nothing to do with the unity of object and subject... consciousness of the past is a constituent part of the historic process. Man has in fact no past unless he is conscious of having one.'[1]

We may make Aron's point in a somewhat different way, which removes from the matter the suspicion that the distinction is a subjective one, dependent merely on man's consciousness. We may say that a past event which is not remembered is not history. By 'remembered', however, I should include any way in which a past event is connected with the present, whether by traditions, written records, collective or individual memory, or even by being inferred from other evidence as having happened. The emphasis then falls not upon the particular way in which the connexion is made, but upon the *presentness* of the connexion. Thus even written records which lie unused or undeciphered are history only if and when they have some connexion with the present, through being used or deciphered, or even through having some previous connexion with some other event which itself is now connected with the present.

It would thus be idle to enquire whether a past event might be history in the sense of having happened, when it is admittedly not history in the sense of having some connexion with the present. For this connexion to be established there must be some kind of investigation. This

---

the enquiry by speaking of a 'significant' happening is likewise unsatisfactory.

[1] *ibid.*

investigation brings the event into the context of memory in the wide sense in which I am using this term.

For example, if we suppose that you have in your neighbourhood a small hill, which you pass every day as you go about your business, then this hill is nothing more than a protuberance of nature, which has nothing to do with history. But suppose that one day you decide to dig into the hill, and you find that it is in fact a tumulus, a burial mound of some long-forgotten chieftain. The piece of nature now begins to show itself to be a piece of history. By your careful investigations you gradually uncover a story of the past. Before you did this, the hill was just a hill. After you did it, the hill is history. It is now remembered. And it is history in the twofold sense: first, it has specific causal connexions with certain events of the past which you are able to reconstruct with more or less accuracy: there was a Viking earl, say, who sailed down the coast of Scotland, and then was slain in battle by the valiant Scots: a great lord in his own land, hungry for new and better land, and so on. This is your reconstruction of the probabilities which I term *Historie*. But secondly, it is history in the sense that it connects with your own life. In this archaeological enterprise, admittedly, the connexion with your life is tenuous; but it is there. This is the fuller definition of what I term *Geschichte*. We simply cannot speak of the past, of what has happened, unless we can make the present connexion. Unless there is this connexion you are unable to get beyond the purely spectatorial construction which has resulted from your enquiry. But the happenedness of the event must now be recognized as connected by way of the historical investigation with your present relation to it. Its acknowledged pastness can be so acknowledged only so far as it exists now, in your present life. If it is not so acknowledged, then we are still talking about an abstraction, namely, a more complex variation of the spectatorial reconstruction.

The problem of the reality of history now appears fundamentally as what Friedrich Gogarten has called 'the problem of the presentness of the past'.[1] If past history were simply part of a process, like natural occurrences, then we should live simply, like the rest of nature, in an unhistorical present. We need not restrict ourselves to saying, with Aron, that the past only exists in virtue of our consciousness of it. But we may say that on the one hand our present is a historical present only when something past becomes present to us, and on the other hand that the past is something that happens in our present. The *Geschichte*, the happenedness, the past, is certainly not given existence by our recognition of it; but it is recognized as existing only as it appears in the present as a real event.

If we may now apply this analysis to the problem of the historical Jesus, we may first note that there is a necessary connexion between the investigation and the findings of historical criticism on the one hand, and the reality which has happened in the past on the other hand. Without this connexion there would be no reason for supposing that anything happened in the past at all. (Clearly the complex web of tradition is a part of the material which is available for the historical investigation.) But second, this connexion can only be realized in the present, either in the existence of the investigator or of those who understand the results of his investigations. *Historie* without *Geschichte* would remain simply an abstract construct. *Geschichte* without *Historie* is likewise an abstraction. The two meet as a unity in the present. Thus if you confine your task to the investigation of the story of Jesus, so far as that is available, you remain a spectator: you have abstracted yourself (necessarily, for this restricted purpose) from the total historicity. The full

[1] *Ich glaube an den dreieinigen Gott*, pp. 71*f.*

reality of this historicity is accessible to you only in the personal, present engagement, and decision for or against the claim which rises out of his past upon your life. Thus the historical investigation and the reality of what happened in the past are united as a single claim upon you now, pressing you for a decision.

In this way we are able to affirm, each in the way proper to its possibilities, the historical (*historische*) facts as a necessary but approximate construction of the historian's enquiry, the reality of the past event out of which that construction arises, but also the necessity for the third and unifying phase, which in turn is also the past event, but now released from mere pastness in the strength of its own possibility into the present.

This analysis is universally valid. At the same time, with reference to the history of Jesus, it is in its particularity different from any other analysis of events. First, it is universally valid. By this I mean that there is no formal difference between the way in which we apprehend, or are encountered by, the past of Jesus and any other past person or event in history. All historical apprehension partakes of this twofold and paradoxical nature. That is to say, any historical event whatever is composed of these two elements, the first being the sheer factuality of its having happened, which is ascertained (approximately, not absolutely) by scientific investigation, and the second being the reality of that happening as present to you. History may therefore be summarily described as what happens to you. But this 'happening' is not an extract from a natural process which may in some sense be described as merely happening (and incidentally, perhaps, to you) such as the sunrise. For the happening to you of a historical event happens as part of a continuing dialogue between your present and the whole of the past which is accessible to you. It is this dialogical

86

element, the dialogic of history, which is paramount. Neither the event as a separate entity of the past, nor your own self as the perceiving subject, may be extracted from this dialogic and given the pre-eminence. The schema of object and subject is not adequate to the dynamic unity of this situation. The reality of the past is therefore a reality of your present. It is not enough to say that two entities with a separate and autonomous existence, a past event on the one hand and your present apprehension of it on the other hand, come into a temporary and accidental unity. Of course the thing must have happened, and it must also mean something to you now. But these two assertions are essentially abstractions from the single unitary situation of the presence of the past event in your situation.

If we may attempt to illustrate the matter by the classic statement that 'Caesar crossed the Rubicon', the temporal sequence is certainly that the causal connexions between the various factors in this event must first be investigated and understood as scientifically as possible. Then it must be recognized that these connexions are nugatory and abstract unless you are able to recognize in the event, or constellation of events to which they refer, a reality which presses upon you now. In this particular example, admittedly, this reality is not easy to analyze and assess. We might say that it comprehends the whole matter of the influence of Roman law and order upon your own present sense of responsibility. But however difficult to define, the event is real in this way, as entering the present. The reality of Caesar's crossing of the Rubicon exists in your present relation to it, and there only, as a reality claiming your decision about one aspect of the way in which you understand your life and its meaning, and thus, of course, its future direction.

If this event were not thus accepted in the continuing

dialogue of history by some members of society in the present, and if in a similar way all events of the past were to slip into oblivion, and be no longer recognized as rising out of the past to encounter us in the way appropriate to their nature, then we should be, as a society, moving along the rough road through barbarism to the nothingness of natural existence, without past, or present, or future.

But secondly, this analysis in its reference to the history of Jesus is in its particularity different from any other analysis of past events. Why is this so? For an answer to this question we must turn to the problem of the eschatological significance of Jesus.

3. History and eschatology

Eschatology in the language of traditional theology is concerned with the study of the 'last things', with death, judgment, heaven and hell. Traditionally these themes have been regarded almost as an afterthought to the main dogmatic propositions.

A typical example of this is Schlatter's *Das Christliche Dogma*,[1] in other respects by no means following the conventional pattern, but in this point entirely in line with tradition. Out of some 550 pages less than 30 are devoted to what Schlatter entitles 'the fulfilment promised to us'.

He begins with a methodological qualm, whether eschatology should not be simply excluded from theology altogether. For, he says, 'Thoughts which describe the future unavoidably possess uncertainty. They are qualitatively different from thoughts which have arisen in us through the complete processes shaped by our experiences. These latter contain certainty and demonstrability on account of their being founded on factual happening.' Whereas the content of eschatology comes from our hope, and so does not possess the same firmness of knowledge.[2] Nevertheless, he goes on, eschatology must come into theology, as otherwise it would be handed over to our fantasy. And so he is free to proceed to the traditional themes, which he develops

[1] Second edition, 1923.   [2] p. 525.

along the twofold line of individual eternal life and of universal promise expressed in the second coming of Christ, this twofold promise being united by the idea of resurrection.

In contrast to this traditional procedure, interpreting it rather than opposing or eliminating it, there is another way of understanding eschatology.

This other way does not regard the 'last things' as items in a doctrinal system, which may be ranged as the objects of hope apart from the firm dogmatic findings arising from our present experiences. But it takes its rise in the actuality of the relationship of faith to God. That faith is a relationship with God means that in anything we say about God we are simultaneously saying something about man. Faith exists in the real mutuality of this relationship. That is to say, it exists in time and space, in historical life. We have no other way of existing than here where we are. Temporality and historicity are the ineluctable conditions of human existence, so thoroughly so, indeed, that it is not enough to say merely that we are in time and history: but we are temporal and historical beings through and through. We know no other way of existing than this, so that even hope can only be known and expressed in temporal and historical terms.

The traditional attempts to express the reality of human existence in other terms are to be understood as attempts to express man's sense that nevertheless, though he is thus bound to time and history, his life is something more than a transient, passing thing. Thus we have the great affirmations concerning the reality of the supranatural as contrasted with the natural world, of eternity as contrasted with time, of the suprahistorical realm which is transcendent to the historical realm, and so on. In these great oppositions it is possible to see man's concern for the meaning of his existence. In the context of such oppositions it is clear that an attempt is being made to understand the fulfilment of man's life as in some sense discontinuous with, even in opposition to, his temporal, intra-mundane, historical existence. But in all these traditional formulations there lurks one grave difficulty, which we may briefly describe as the docetic problem. If our life has meaning only in a realm which is in one way or the other discontinuous with or opposed to this world of time and history, how are we to succeed in taking this present world seriously? Is our temporal and historical life just a semblance? And is the real life still to come, in heaven, or in the suprahistorical and supranatural realm, the transcendent and eternal kingdom of God?

I shall not attempt a direct critique of these great and honoured formulations. This would mean an attempt to assess the whole course of philosophical thinking since the Greeks. What I wish rather to do is to ask the question concerning man's existence in terms of the historicity of Jesus. Faith in Jesus is through and through eschatological: the eschatology is not an afterthought, to take care of the unknown beyond history, regarded as happening by God's action at the end of time or beyond time. Nor is the eschatology of the New Testament to be confined to a description of an expectation concerning the near coming of that end. Certainly, the terms of Jewish apocalyptic did give rise to this expectation of the imminence of that end, and it has been one of the grave problems not only of New Testament exegesis but also of the whole of the history of the church how to come to terms with the fact that that expectation of an imminent fulfilment did not take place. But it is in any case no real solution of this problem merely to regard that fulfilment as postponed for a while, or until some indefinite future described as 'the end of time'. The real significance of the eschatological attitude of the New

Testament is expressed neither in the straightforward mythological forms of apocalyptic nor in some pseudo-rational but still mythological formulation like 'the end of time'. But its significance is to be understood in terms of the particular relationship of faith to God and to the world.

This relationship is constituted by the temporal, historical event of Christ. He is the end, he is the Last One, not in the sense of being the goal of historical development, or the ideal who is to be realized by or in the historical process, but in the sense that he already is the end: in his life history has come to an end. This is true in a twofold sense, which derives from the twofold reality of his life and death. This historical reality is a paradoxical union of the free action of Jesus and the free giving of the Father. On the one hand this life of Jesus is a free movement towards his death: he lays down his life of himself,[1] and in this free movement we see the historical outcome of the life of this world. This outcome is death. That this life of Jesus comes to death, through forsakenness by all men, and by God, is the judgment upon this world.

On the other hand this life is the free giving of God to men of his own reality: a giving which is a forgiving. The end which is reached by the death of Jesus is thus also a beginning—in the same death. Thus the Cross is the symbol both of the suffering and the action of God.

That we may thus speak of the Cross as symbolizing the suffering and the action of God is certainly paradoxical. It is paradoxical in that we recognize and confess in the Cross of Jesus the judgment of God upon all history. It is paradoxical in that in the Cross of Jesus as the Christ we recognize and confess the forgiving action of God extended to all history. We recognize and confess that human history by itself ends there: its only end is death: 'for they are all

[1] John 10.18.

given over to death, to the nether world among mortal men, with those who go down to the Pit.'[1] But simultaneously we recognize and confess that a new beginning to history is made. By itself, then, within itself, history has at best only relative significance, a significance which runs out in the absolute nothingness of Christ's cry of dereliction from the Cross: 'My God, my God, why hast thou forsaken me?"[2] Only when it has thus run out in nothingness, and the judgment upon it is accepted, may the judgment be seen to be also forgiveness: seen, that is *believed* as the reality of Christ's life and death. And in the believing acceptance of this forgiveness history is renewed.

If it is asked, 'On what grounds do you make these assertions? Or where do you see the confirming signs of this judgment and this renewal?' then the only answer can be that this is what I confess: this is my faith: this is the way I understand my life, and the death of the old possibilities, and the meaning of the possibilities in the event of Jesus as the Christ. There are no grounds outside the trusting acceptance of the message concerning him, which I receive from the very material of his history. This history includes not only what we may learn of the historical actuality of his life within the context of normal world history (his *Historie*), but also the claim which this life makes upon my own life, exposing both its futility and its new possibility (his *Geschichte*). Out of the despair, the disaster, and the death which are the concomitants of his life, as they are in their way of my own, there arises the faith, which is the other side of the despair, the disaster and the death, that nevertheless there is hope, restoration, and life.

This is both the form and the content—so far as the content can be described in general terms—of the eschatological event of Christ. Thus history, which has no absolute

[1]Ezekiel 31.14.   [2]Mark 15.34.

meaning in itself, is given meaning: the meaning of the personal reality of persistent forgiveness.

This, then, is what I term the pervasive eschatological significance of the New Testament message. This eschatological significance can therefore not be confined to the 'end' of history, conceived of as the near or distant winding-up of the scheme of things, whether this is conceived of as a 'process' or an 'organic development' or even as a *Heilsgeschichte*' or redemptive history, somehow imposed upon, or parallel to, or transparent through, the ordinary immanent course of events. For the message concerning Jesus is that the reality of the end to this immanent course of events has already been completed in the life and death of Jesus. The judgment has already come: 'this is the judgment, that the light has come into the world, and men loved darkness rather than light, because their deeds were evil.'[1] In this sense the eschatology is thoroughly and completely realized. In another sense, however, it is not yet realized, because it is to be realized again and again in the life of the individual believer. Thus the eschatological fulfilment in the life and death of Jesus is fulfilled precisely in its constantly recurrent bearing upon each present time, pointing to the real future that is thereby opened for each present time. Without this recurring renewal of realization and fulfilment the life and death of Jesus would once more be misconceived as a docetic exercise requiring for its legitimation a mythological guarantee. His life and death would then have at most the character of a declaration that human history, the immanent course of events, was without reality, whereas only God in heaven has reality. But the eschatological reality of the life and death of Jesus means that the historical course of events is not simply condemned and written off. The history of each single person may be taken up into this

[1]John 3.19.

reality. So just because of the final and conclusive reality of the life and death of Jesus, as completely realizing God's loving, forgiving renewal of men, there is still this sense in which everything is not completed. But it must be emphasized that this does not mean that the triumph of God in Christ has somehow to be added to, or carried out in a new or a really final way, say in some return of Christ, however conceived. This would be a conception of Christ as the eschatological event which had left the personal realm and responsible historical action in favour of an objectifying view, couched in mythological language, which would essentially negate the whole message. To put it another way, such a misconception, which tried to express the reality of Christ's action and suffering for the world in terms which as it were left something undone, and still to be done, would make of his life and death merely a heroic, entirely relative, immanent and tragic action: indeed, no more than a human gesture.

But what is in truth left is the time of God's patience with men, the future which he offers in which men may find in faith the way to confirm that nevertheless there is meaning.

This time that is left is neither an interim nor an aftermath. It is not an interim, a time between two great times, the time of Christ's first coming and the time of his second coming. For to speak in this way is on the one hand to restore the conception of an immanent *Heilsgeschichte*, an observable drama of which we are mere spectators; and on the other hand it is to diminish the historicity of Christ's life and death. And both these consequences would serve to evacuate this time that is left of its reality.

And it is not an aftermath, for such a description, too, would leave the believer outside of the eschatological event. He would then have to depend on the dramatic persuasiveness of such illusory metaphors as Oscar Cullmann's when he speaks of the life of Christ as D-day, and the time since then as the time of mopping-up operations before V-day.[1] But we must insist that the time that is left to the world is in truth the time that God has given. It is the same fulfilled time in which Christ came, and lived, and died. This time that is left is thus God's *now*—'Now is the accepted time, now is the day of salvation'; 'Now is the judgment of this world.'[2] For faith there is only this one time, which is the time of Christ's suffering and action. The eschatological event which is Christ's life may therefore be described as the possibility given by God which may again and again be realized in faith.

Christ as the eschatological event is thus not only the reality of the New Testament kerygma, in the light of which every part of the New Testament is illumined and set in its true perspective. He also engenders faith as a way of existence which is itself eschatological. And just as Christ puts an end to history, as an immanent and self-contained course of events, and exposes it as a rushing upon death, so for faith history is at an end. The man of faith has been taken out of the world, *'entweltlicht'*. He no longer lives with himself in the world, but in faith he has passed through judgment into life.

And what is this life into which he has passed? It is not a state of being, or a possession, any more than the resurrection which is the symbol of this new life is a state of being or a possession.

But for the meaning of the resurrection we must begin a new chapter.

---

[1] See his *Christ and Time*, London, 1951, pp. 39, 84.
[2] 2 Corinthians 6.2; John 12.31.

4. *The resurrection*

I have just spoken of the resurrection of Christ as 'the symbol of the new life' into which in faith we may enter. But I said that the new life is not a state of being or a possession any more than the resurrection is a state of being or a possession.

In calling the resurrection the symbol of the new life I mean that it is a way of affirming the forgiving act of God in Christ. In denying that it may be described as a state of being or a possession I mean that it can neither be affirmed as an objective happening nor incorporated as a fact within the structure of the church's faith.

It may at once be objected that this looks very like a reduction of the resurrection to a mere mode of my own existence. And must one not, on the contrary, affirm that the resurrection is a historical fact, proved by the empty grave, confirmed by the appearances of Jesus after his death to the disciples, and carried forward as the triumphant act of God in the transformed lives of the disciples, and so down through the whole life of the church? Is it not, in brief, the *articulus stantis et cadentis* of the church, as St Paul indicates when he writes, 'If Christ has not been raised then our preaching is in vain and your faith is in vain'?[1]

We may certainly agree that without faith in the Risen

[1] 1 Corinthians 15.14.

Christ there would be no church, no continuing relation to God through Christ. But in the light of what we have already said, both about our own relation to scripture and about the way in which past events may be present to us, it is necessary to ask more precisely in what way we may be grasped by the truth of the resurrection.

Our answer to this question must be in terms of the position we have step by step reached, in our whole consideration of the nature of faith and the nature of history.

It is not my intention to attempt to write a theology of the resurrection. Such an attempt is indeed precluded by the way we have so far gone. The resurrection cannot be isolated from the whole event of Christ. Amid the immense confusion of voices in modern theology about the resurrection, we do not propose to do more here than establish a few basic positions. If this seems naive, in contrast with the sophistication of so much of the present-day work of the New Testament scholars, I can only say that it is only by a clear statement of the presuppositions of thought and of the whole context of the matter that we may hope to overcome the confusion and reach a reasonable conclusion.

To take first the matter of our relation to scripture, we must repeat that since the Enlightenment the work of critical scholarship has gone forward in a way that is on a different plane from that of the early church. Our understanding of our relation to the past now appears as both more complex and clearer than that even of the writers of the New Testament. We simply cannot circumvent the distinctions we have drawn between the construction of the past which may be elicited by historical investigation (*Historie*) and the real happenedness (*Geschichte*) of a past event. Nor, further, can we separate these two elements in our completed understanding of them. This understanding, as I have said, takes the form of a happening:

it is as presentness, as one part of the dialogic of history, that past events are accessible to us. Certainly without *Historie*, some form of remembered past, there can be no *Geschichte*, no past reality: but it is the two together which constitute the unity of the dialogical partner in my present.

Secondly, in terms of this analysis of history we have already spoken of the eschatological reality of the life and death of Jesus: this is the message concerning Christ, that we in our present lives may be confronted by his reality in such a way that we may enter into a new life. This may indeed be called the 'resurrection life', in virtue of the *eschaton* which is reached through the judgment and the forgiveness offered in his eschatological reality. But this resurrection life is constituted by the relation of faith which is made possible for us by his whole historical reality present to us now in its focused power.

We must therefore say that we cannot separate the resurrection from the crucifixion. That is to say, we cannot separate it from the life and death of Jesus. That is further to say that we cannot speak of the resurrection unconnected with the historical sources and the construction (the *Historie*) which may be made from these sources. If the resurrection were regarded as an addition to the *Historie* in the sense of a *bouleversement* of the life and death of Jesus we should in fact be departing from the historical material. Certainly, the accounts we have show a transformation in the disciples. But this transformation is basically one of faith. Their faith in God is established as a faith through the life and death of Jesus. This life and death are now recognized not as a meaningless catastrophe, which is then over-whelmed, so to speak, by an act of *force majeure* on the part of God, namely, the resurrection. But their faith in God is established in and through the death of Christ as God's conclusive act.

If we attempt to separate off the resurrection from the life and death of Christ, then we are committed to a view of God's dealing with men which is not a judgment upon man's self-assertion and his despair, and in this way a forgiving and renewal of man. But in that case the resurrection would be conceived as something much more like an act of despair in itself, as though God were forced to write off not only all previous history, but also the history of Christ's life and death, by an action which bears no conceivable relation to history. If this were the reality of the resurrection, then we should be committing ourselves to the acceptance of an action which is sheerly unhistorical, and therefore strictly speaking nonsense. And no matter the terms in which this action were then described, no matter the exalted tones which accompanied the description, its inability to make sense of any of our historical categories, its basic non-sense, would turn Christianity into sheer incredibility. On my view any attempt to describe the resurrection as 'supra-historical', or 'supernatural', as 'trans-historical' or 'metahistorical', as the 'second primal miracle' (as Künneth calls it[1]), or as belonging to '*Geschichte*' but with only 'a narrow historical (*historische*) verge' (as Karl Barth says[2])—any such description partakes of the same inability to make sense. That is, such descriptions do not make sense adequate to the historical reality of the message concerning Christ as the eschatological event.

Thus when Karl Barth writes that 'One could think of a New Testament which contained only the Easter story and the Easter message, but not of a New Testament without them,'[3] I can only regard this as a polemical and senseless

---

[1] Walther Künneth, *Theologie der Auferstehung* [4], pp. 63 *ff.*

[2] Karl Barth, *Kirchliche Dogmatik*, III/2, p. 535. *Cf.* Eng. trans., *Church Dogmatics*, III/2, p. 446.

[3] *op. cit.*, p. 531. Cf. *Church Dogmatics*, III/2, p. 442.

exaggeration. For the resurrection is a reality as an expression of the historical being of God for men in Christ. That is, faith in God's being for men is expressed in the affirmation of the Risen Christ. But the resurrection by itself, regarded as an expression of God's victory over death, would be a mere denial of that historical being. A New Testament which contained only the Easter story and the Easter message would be a fairy-tale. It is only when the Easter message is seen as integrated with the historical life of Jesus that it may be believed as the meaning of that life. And by the historical life of Jesus, let me repeat, I mean the unity of his historical (*historische*) existence, as that may be derived from an assessment of the New Testament writings, with the reality of that history in its presence to us in the message itself (the *Geschichte*).

Now the resurrection cannot be described in simple factual terms. The New Testament does not do this. There is no *Historie* possible for the resurrection as an isolated 'fact'. For attempts along this line we have to turn to the apocryphal and uncanonical so-called *Gospel of Peter*. There indeed we may read an attempted version of the resurrection as an occurrence available to the objective spectator. According to M. R. James, 'it is not safe to date the book much earlier than 150 A.D.'[1] It is worth quoting the central part of the narrative, as M. R. James has translated it from a fragment discovered in a tomb in Egypt in 1884:

And early in the morning as the sabbath dawned, there came a multitude from Jerusalem and the region round about to see the sepulchre that had been sealed.

Now in the night whereon the Lord's day dawned, as the soldiers were keeping guard two by two in every watch, there came a great sound in the heaven, and they saw the heavens opened and two men descend

[1] M. R. James, *The Apocryphal New Testament*, p. 90.

thence, shining with (*lit.* having) a great light, and drawing near unto the sepulchre. And that stone which had been set on the door rolled away of itself and went back to the side, and the sepulchre was opened and both of the young men entered in. When therefore those soldiers saw *that*, they waked up the centurion and the elders (for they also were there keeping watch); and while they were *yet* telling them the things which they had seen, they saw again three men come out of the sepulchre, and two of them sustaining the other (*lit.* the one), and a cross following after them. And of the two they saw that their heads reached unto heaven, but of him that was led by them that it overpassed the heavens. And they heard a voice out of the heavens: Hast thou (*or* Thou hast) preached unto them that sleep? And an answer was heard from the cross, *saying*: Yea.[1]

The stories of the empty tomb, as we find them in the canonical gospels, do not reach the extreme which the *Gospel of Peter* describes with such pathos and drama. Nevertheless, they partake of the same legendary quality. Even Karl Barth admits the ambiguous and contestable nature of the 'fact', and is ready to call it a legend, but a legend as part of the 'saga' concerning the living Jesus which must be retained as a 'sign'.[2] We must rather say that the accounts of the empty tomb in the gospels, so far as they imply an 'objective' fact of the resurrection, are mythologizing legends. Regarded as a form in which the faith in the risen Lord is expressed (and embellished), their status as part of the kerygma or message of faith to faith is clear. Unfortunately, however, there is an immense and constant temptation at this point to elevate the legends of the empty

[1] *ibid.*, pp. 92*f.*
[2] *Kirchliche Dogmatik*, III/2, pp. 543*f.* Cf. *Church Dogmatics*, III/2, p. 453.

tomb (and in a similar way the stories of the appearances of Jesus, and the mythological account of the ascension) into the separate status of objective 'happenings'.

'Legend' and 'sign' only connect with the kerygma in the context of faith. So far as historicity is concerned, *historische* fact, it is necessary to be plain: we may freely say that the bones of Jesus lie somewhere in Palestine.

Christian faith is not destroyed by this admission. On the contrary, only now, when this has been said, are we in a position to ask about the meaning of the resurrection as an integral part of the message concerning Jesus.

The reality of Jesus with which we have to do in faith at this point is not an irrational addendum to his whole life. We are not asked to believe in the empty tomb, or in the resurrection: but in the living Lord. So far as the histori-cally ascertainable 'facts' are concerned, we have the faith of the disciples, nothing more. They believed in the reality of the Risen Lord. They believed in this because they believed in his life and death as the forgiving action of God. No sacrifice of the intellect is demanded at this point. The real *skandalon* is not that we are asked to accept as a verifiable piece of 'history' (*Historie*) an anti-historical dramatic intervention of God in the form of a miraculous sign, namely, the raising from the dead. But the *skandalon*, the stumbling-block, is that we are invited to believe that here in the life and the death of a man God has entered into man's historical existence and in this life and this death has acted out his own being, as a being for men and not against them, judging them in their self-contained pretensions, and for-giving them, not giving them over to the logical end of their existence, in meaninglessness, futility, death, and nothingness.

So the *skandalon* of Christianity is neither supra-historical nor anti-historical; but it is supremely historical. It confronts us in our present in the paradoxical union of the historical actuality of a man's life and death, an actuality which may be constated by historical investigation, and the conclusive reality of that life as the historical reality of God. Therefore just as we cannot rely on the historical investigation alone, similarly we cannot rely on what I have called the 'conclusive reality' of that life in separation from the historical probabilities. That is to say, we cannot rely on something that purports to be 'real' history in separation from the historically accessible message of the life and death.

The resurrection, therefore, is a way of affirming the forgiving purpose of God in the historical reality of the life of Christ.

It might still be asked whether I do not wish to try to combine two impossible things. On the one hand I wish to abandon the objective factual reality of the empty tomb; and on the other hand I wish to retain the certainty which is traditionally regarded as the accompaniment of that factual reality. Am I not trying to have the best of two incompatible worlds, the world of God's triumphant action, and the world of common human sense, where such irrational things as the resuscitation of a corpse simply do not happen? As Karl Barth asks, rhetorically, 'Why should it [the Easter history—*Geschichte*] not therefore have happened? It is sheer superstition to suppose that only what is historically (*historisch*) ascertainable can really happen in time. There could be happenings which happened much more certainly in time than all that the historian as such could ascertain.'[1] To this rhetorical question I can only reply that this is not the way the conclusive reality of Christ is presented to us. It is not presented to us in the form of a demand for assent to an immediately accessible 'fact', namely, the resurrected body of Jesus, evidenced by the

[1] *op. cit.*, p. 535. Cf. *Church Dogmatics*, III/2, p. 446.

empty tomb, the appearances, and so on. Such a demand would be an invitation to 'sheer superstition'.

The real alternative is not between refusing faith and accepting the 'objective fact' of the resurrection, but between faith and unbelief in face of the message concerning Jesus. Faith affirms the real presence of God in the life and death of Jesus, with all its consequences. Unbelief refuses this affirmation. It is unbelief which presses for a miracle.

We might well ask, what is it that the would-be orthodox hope to prove by insisting upon an object of faith in terms of a visible, bodily, attestable resurrection? Can it be anything but a substitute for faith, a theophany which removes all ambiguity? Such a desire destroys the basic historicity of faith. For faith consists in the affirmation of God's historical self-giving in Christ. This does not involve the sacrifice of the intellect. Rather the intellect here willingly yields its pretensions, at the limit of its possibilities. It is not overthrown by a miracle which 'subverts all the principles of reason'. But it is given its powers back again to be exercised in their fulness in the confrontation by the sheer goodness of God.

There is a certainty of faith which is, however, different from the relative and approximate certainty which is all that can be affirmed of any given causal connexions in past events. The certainty of faith is the affirmation of meaning in that life of self-giving which is Christ's. But because it is an affirmation of faith it is an uncertain certainty, or, in Luther's splendid words, 'a fighting certainty'.

To attempt to transpose this affirmation into a realm of objective certainty, even if this realm claims the sanction of God's sovereign power, is an affirmation not of faith but of incredulity and despair; and, ultimately, of disbelief in the reality of history. It does no honour to the triumphant glory of God's goodness, and to his humble presence in the midst of history, in Christ, to conceive of his power as an arbitrary imposition. If we hold by the Christian kerygma we are bound to say that God expresses himself historically in terms of powerlessness, the powerlessness of love which has no other way of expressing itself than the way of the Cross. Even if we hold that God's power may be expressed directly and absolutely, we are bound to say that the way he has in fact expressed himself can only be described as a withholding of that power. Omnipotence is not directly accessible. God's only way of being, as historically available in the reality of faith, is the way of powerless self-giving.

5. *History and Heilsgeschichte*

So far, in this section on history, I have pointed out the central place which the concept of history takes in theology today, in a fashion which became explicit only with the Enlightenment. Arising as it did in the study of the biblical documents, it has had revolutionary effects upon the whole approach to the thought-world of the biblical writers. It has also had striking effects upon the way in which history may be understood as the very reality in which God and man come together. This led to a consideration of the historical Jesus, and to the limitations of a study which was restricted to the scientific-literary-historical, what the Germans call the *historische*, element in the life of Jesus. The ambiguity in the term 'history' was then analysed in the light of the distinction between the results of so-called historical investigation (*Historie*) and the reality of the past (*Geschichte*). But this distinction does not imply a severance. In fact the two elements constitute together the paradoxical unity which can be encountered in any and every so-called past event—so far as that event is able to make a claim upon us in our present historical existence. From this universal consideration I returned to the problem of the history of Jesus: and here the paradoxical combination of the results of historical investigation and the reality of past events encounters us as the eschatological reality. By this I mean that in and through the message concerning

Jesus, as conveyed to us through the biblical records, we are faced with the ultimate question concerning the meaning of our existence. This is a confrontation of faith. That is, we are asked for an answer to the question raised by the history of Jesus which is not based upon any prior assertion, whether of the meaning of the world as a whole or the achievements of our own life. In this history of Jesus, in the message concerning him, we are faced with an absolute demand. We are asked to believe that here we face an end to all our efforts. And this end is by no means simple. For it is simultaneously a judgment upon the whole course of history, and the course of our own life, judging them as hopeless and leading only to death, and a forgiveness of all that we, and by implication the whole intra-mundane course of events, both are and have brought about. This is the heart of the meaning of 'eschatological', of the eschatological event of Christ and of the eschatological possibility which is now open, both to each of us personally, and to the whole course of history. Nothing less than a total commitment to a new life, for each single person and for all human history, is here implicated. This is the grand dialogic of history which is to be found, concentrated and focused, in the message concerning Christ. History, after all, is given a meaning. Our life is given a meaning. Judged and forgiven, we are set on a new way.

It was in the context of these reflections that I then came to speak of the resurrection of Christ. I was unable to describe the reality of Christ's demand upon us in the naive terms of a miracle which simply bowled us over. The real miracle remains the Word become flesh. This is not to be understood as an unambiguous theophany. Nor is it to be seen as an exercise of arbitrary power on the part of God. The mystery in which God clothes his condescensions towards man is not set aside in the resurrection. But he speaks all the time indirectly, he is incognito, he is not directly seen or apprehended. This holds true of the resurrection as well. So it is necessary to be quite candid concerning the Gospel accounts: so far as they seem to express direct, by means of the so-called 'fact' of the empty tomb and the appearances of Jesus, the eschatological reality of Christ's history as the judging and forgiving action of God, as the end and the beginning for all history, they are either being misunderstood or they themselves misunderstand the very reality of which they speak. The alternative, however, is not the last word: for with our very different view of history and our very different conceptuality it is incumbent upon us neither simply to try to think the evangelists' thoughts after them nor to abandon them, but to re-think them in our own history.

If we may return, by way of further illustration of this point, to the account which St Paul gives in I Corinthians 15.3–8 of the appearances of Jesus, we may indeed recognize that Paul is attempting to legitimize the resurrection by means of the direct evidence of the senses: he adds himself as the last in a series by whom the Lord 'was seen'. He is presumably referring to his experience on the Damascus road. St Paul simply does not tell us what the nature of the Lord's 'being seen' by the others really was. But his own experience has certainly to be set in the context of his whole understanding of the reality of his Lord. He is bearing witness, here as elsewhere, to the faith which he has been given in the kerygma. He is pointing to the reality by which he now lives in faith.

What is therefore incumbent upon us is to recognize that the moment of the resurrection cannot be separated from the way in which God made himself known in the life of Christ. This does not mean a simple return (which is in any case impossible) to the 'Christ after the flesh'. But it does mean that we may recognize in faith that the whole life of Christ is one of powerless love. Against the self-assertion of the world God has only one reaction, and that is the reaction of utter, unadulterated, suffering self-giving. Thus the resurrection is wrongly described as a stone of stumbling for the intellect, in the sense that the reason is here invited to capitulate before an arbitrary exercise of power. But the resurrection is truly an offence in the sense that the man who is confronted with the life and death of Christ is required to decide whether he is ready to live his life henceforth in the old jog-trot of his own self-assertion, or in the new style offered to him in Christ. This is an offence because it leaves no room for all that can be described as the man's own achievement. (The dialectic which is inherent in this situation, by which there nevertheless is achievement, and even the possibility of goodness, will be discussed later, when we face the problem of secularism.)

It is in this context, then, that we now face the problem of so-called *Heilsgeschichte*. *Heilsgeschichte* means literally the story, or the history, of redemption, or salvation history. This description of what has been done for us by God in Christ has highly respectable antecedents. It is to be found in the New Testament, especially in the apocalyptic view of eschatology. It reached its high point in the historical analysis of St Augustine, where we see the *civitas terrena* set in ambiguous conflict with the *civitas eterna*. Put crudely, this view is that in the whole of human history we may see certain selected moments as the dramatic, observable, and demonstrable intervention of God in man's history. The mighty acts of God, as they are called in the Old Testament, are manifest as the expression of his purpose with man. These mighty acts are regarded as breaking the continuity of history, plunging vertically down into the horizontal course of history, and causing in man who is their recipient the submission of the creature to the wonderful acts of the Creator. The basic presupposition is that man is a spectator of the wondrous actions of God. Faced with them, he can only bow his head, and adore.

It is doubtful whether the sense of what Rudolf Otto has called 'the numinous' is able to play any dominant part in the life of modern man. Even if the *frisson* in face of the uncanny is still possible, it is doubtful whether the experience may be isolated and given the status which is sometimes desired for it by proponents of a religious revival. Certainly, the conventional idea of the story of redemption which is its notional counterpart does not do justice to the reality of Christ's life. It is not possible to fit that life into a scheme of thought which would regard it as one moment, even as the supreme moment, in which God may be observed dealing with men. The reality of that life is not observable at all. It is not to be grasped as an object within the succession of objects in the world, and it can therefore neither be used for the purpose of confirming and fulfilling, nor for the purpose of breaking, the sequence or flow of mighty acts. It can only be understood as the fulfilment of the story of Israel in the sense that as that story is one of disobedience and failure, so the story of Jesus is the culminating illustration of the disobedience of Israel and therefore of failure on the part of Jesus as well. And it can only be understood as the breaking of the sequence of events in the sense that the events are here both judged and forgiven. The conventional notion of *Heilsgeschichte* is shattered by the death of Christ on the cross.

The basic defect of the conventional idea of *Heilsgeschichte* is that it emphasizes (as Professor McIntyre has said) *Heil* at the expense of *Geschichte*. The cross becomes an unhistorical and docetic triumph. The view ignores the way in which all men are necessarily placed in history, embedded in history, in such a way that they *are* history, and in such a way that history is what happens to them and is their understanding of what life is. But this view of *Heilsgeschichte*, ignoring history, goes on to assume many different forms of self-explanation: it becomes super-history, or transhistorical, or it points to a timeless truth, or it takes refuge in sheer miracle: the reality is God in his dramatic interventions, and everything else is reduced to unreality. Christian faith becomes a mere superstitious addendum to the incredible miracle. Christianity is then equivalent to credulity, believing that 'something impossible really happened'.

Thus the theory of *Heilsgeschichte* is that God intervenes, against reason and against the historicity of man, with a miracle that compels obedience; and that in the sequence of miraculous acts preceding and consequent upon the life of Jesus, as well as in the similarly outlined life of Jesus, we have the real story of mankind—in other words, a story of supreme arbitrariness, of sovereign indifference to the whole sweep of human history, and of a sublime reduction of all that man has done to a handful of selected 'moments', objectifiably certifiable, in the peculiar story of Israel.

This view of the life of man, and in particular of the life of Christ, goes clean contrary to all that we may learn from the bible itself both of Christ and of man's relation to him in faith. The view of eschatology which is implied here is of a specific future conclusion to God's action in the world, which began with the creation and leads through biblical history to the end of the ages. I have called this view trans-historical because it thinks of a series of events which are analogous to ordinary world-historical happenings, at least in the sense that they can be observed and put in chrono-logical order, analysed for their causal status and recognized as moving purposively towards their end. But at the same time they are supranatural events. Man shares in them only like 'a passenger who shares in the course of a ship moving along a river',[1] or he has been rescued from the stream of ordinary history by an ideological ark which rides high above the world.

It is important to notice that behind this view of salvation history there lies the hidden presupposition that being is to be realized as a continual development or progress towards an objectively visible conclusion. The nineteenth century positivist and evolutionary theory of history, which found classic expression in the thought of Hegel, has been surreptitiously taken over in this view, and transposed to fit the biblical story. Thus an immensely arbitrary operation is carried out on the biblical faith in Christ, with the result that salvation history is picked out as the only real expression of this steady progress towards a given goal. Then from this standpoint the rest of history is interpreted in terms of blessing or curse, according as it fits this preselected scheme.

In our time the work of Oscar Cullmann, *Christ and Time*, is an excellent illustration of this view of salvation history, backed up as it is by a massive exegetical operation. Cullmann works with the primitive Jewish apocalyptic view as it is reflected in the New Testament. From this starting-point he reaches a view of time which he regards as generally applicable in the New Testament. In this view God's redemptive action is regarded as taking place in the sequence of events along the line of time. It began in the breadth of universal history, then narrowed down to Israel, first as the chosen people, and then as rejected, till it reaches the mid-point of all history, namely, Christ, from

[1]Johannes Körner, *Eschatologie und Geschichte*, p. 64. I owe much stimulus to Körner's thorough study of the meaning of eschatology, both in its New Testament form and in the wider *geistesgeschichtliche* context.

where it broadens out again through the church to its fulfilment in the second coming of Christ. The selective principle
and the optimistic mythological interpretation are fashionable in our time, as witness, for instance the widely ac-
claimed historical studies of Kenneth Scott Latourette,
A History of the Expansion of Christianity, and the like.

Cullmann's futurist eschatology can certainly appeal to
many passages in the New Testament, especially in the
Synoptic Gospels and in St Paul, where this view comes into
sight. Thus we read in Matthew 24.36: 'But of that day
and hour no one knows, not even the angels of heaven, nor
the Son, but the Father only.' And in Mark 9.1 we read:
'Truly I say to you, there are some standing here who will
not taste death before they see the kingdom of God come
with power.' And St Paul, in I Thessalonians 4.16: 'For
the Lord himself will descend from heaven with a cry of
command, with the archangel's call, and with the sound of
the trumpet of God . . .'; and in Romans 13.11: 'Besides
this you know what hour it is, how it is full time now for
you to wake from sleep. For salvation is nearer to us now
than when we first believed; the night is far gone, the day
is at hand.'

The writings of John, on the other hand, indicate an
entirely different view of the relation of salvation to time
and to history. Here the crucifixion itself is seen as the
exaltation, which includes resurrection, ascension and
fellowship. 'Now is the judgment of this world . . . and I,
when I am lifted up from the earth, will draw all men to
myself.'[1] 'To abide in him' is the already present eschatological reality. Certainly there is a clear sense, even in the
Johannine writings, in which there is a 'not yet', something
still to be fulfilled. Thus we read: 'Father, I desire that they
also, whom thou hast given me, may be with me where I am,

[1] John 12.27*ff.*

114

to behold my glory which thou hast given me in thy love for me before the foundation of the world.'[1] And again: 'Beloved, we are God's children now; it does not yet appear what we shall be, but we know that when he appears we shall be like him, for we shall see him as he is. And every one who thus hopes in him purifies himself as he is pure.'[2] But this permanent hope is basically a hope which is founded upon the present reality. It is not the last of a sequence of observable events, running along a time process. The reality of redemption is presented as the present fulfilment of history. It is the confrontation of man with God in the present which is decisive.

And this must be said of the New Testament view as a whole. The reality of the redemptive event is grounded in the present relation of faith, and not in any futurist view, especially not in any conception of a future state of affairs. Certainly, the sense that there is a reality still to be attained runs through the New Testament. But this is the reality of hope arising out of faith. The mystery of the real presence of Christ to faith is the eschatological reality upon which all Christian faith is based, and by which all views of the nature of God's redemptive action must be judged. We may equally say that it is the faith in this presence which is constitutive of the view of salvation history.

In the light of our discussion of salvation history we must therefore severely modify Karl Barth's assertion that 'the history of the man Jesus is *Heilsgeschichte*'.[3] For this history cannot be understood as an isolated and dramatic interruption of ordinary world history by any 'bolt from the blue', but only as the eschatological reality as we have described it. On the one hand it is not an act which can be interpreted in a positivist fashion, comparable, that is, to the

<hr />

[1]John 17.24.   [2]1 John 3.2.
[3]*Kirchliche Dogmatik*, iii/2, p. 529. Cf. *Church Dogmatics*, iii/2, p. 441.

observable and objectifiable course of events in world history. On the other hand it is not an act which is simply separated from ordinary history as something transhistorical or supranatural. But it is an act which at one and the same time takes the world and time and history entirely seriously, without the least docetic overtones, and puts an end to the world and time and history. There is therefore a real sense in which we can and must speak of the redemptive action of God in Christ. Christ really is God's saving act, the saviour. He is the saviour in that through his life, suffering and death he brings final judgment upon the world, upon its history and expectations, and signs it off with the signature of the cross: and simultaneously, and paradoxically, he inaugurates a new possibility for this same world which is undersigned by death—the possibility of renewal.

But if we are thus able to speak, and indeed find ourselves bound to speak, of the redemptive act of God in Christ, it might well be asked whether after all we are not back in the old mythological world of *Heilsgeschichte* once more. By speaking of an act of God, however narrowly circumscribed, are we not thinking mythologically of some kind of dramatic interruption to ordinary history? Our question now takes the form of asking whether we can really speak of an act of God, or of God acting. What meaning is there in this conception of an act of God?

6. An act of God

When we face the question, What do we really mean by an act of God? the tradition of negative theology is of the utmost importance. This tradition is of course not all that must be invoked. By itself it would be sheer agnosticism. But without this tradition we should find ourselves in danger of speaking about God in terms of pietist familiarity or of a non-committal pantheism, or in terms of mythological formulas which would give us the illusion that we know all about God.

In the tradition of negative theology the basic insight is that God is not of this world. He does not belong to us, and he cannot be expressed by us. So, traditionally, it is asserted that he is not mortal, not visible, not a body or object in the world, not in any sense a part, or extension, of the world at all. He is quite different from the world, and separated from it.

This is an ancient insight, with which we agree. Kierkegaard gave it particular form when he insisted that God is 'qualitatively different'.

But we are not left in mere ignorance. When we try to speak of God we believe that he is simply what he does. When we dare to speak of his acts we mean his acts as the expression of what he is. He does not mock us, or cheat us: he does not pretend to be other than he is. He does not act in one way, and *be* in another way. His being is not separable from his action. If this possibility were to arise seriously, and dominate our action, then it would mean that truth was an illusion. In that case there would be no meaning in life at all, and our actions themselves, and with them all history, would be like a waste-pit into which everything descended in an interminable nightmare of meaninglessness.

But as we base our whole faith on the qualitative difference between God and man, so we must say that we cannot speak *directly* of God in terms of man. That is, his being is neither directly accessible, nor entirely comprehensible. But nevertheless he is accessible in terms of what he does. And what he does—for we believe that he is true—bears the characteristics of what he is. This is both a limiting and a liberating insight of faith. It is limiting, in that what he does is not the directly comprehensible expression of what he is. It is liberating, in that what he does is indeed one with what he is. Thus while we must say that the being of God is apprehensible by us only indirectly, nevertheless what he is is truly apprehensible.

Friedrich Gogarten, who has contributed more than any other modern scholar to the implications of the classic formulations of Martin Buber concerning the nature of personal relations, has the following illuminating remarks on our theme:

The more profoundly I know about a man who gives himself to me in love and trust, the more directly I experience him in this, the more powerful does the mystery which surrounds him become, just because he is a person who reveals himself to me. The more completely and unconditionally he promises himself to me, and the more purely I am able to grasp this, the more profoundly do I also grasp his being-for-himself, out of whose incomprehensible fulness he is there for me.

Thus there is no knowledge of revelation of God without at the same time the knowledge of his eternal hiddenness, just as on the other hand there is no knowledge of this his eternal being-for-himself other than in his being for us.[1]

In our terminology, then, we may say that God is apprehensible only in what he is towards us, that is, in his acts. Behind the acts lies a mysterious hinterland of being. When we speak of God as acting we are therefore speaking in terms of a double indirectness: first, there is the indirectness which necessarily follows from his utter otherness from us; and second, there is the indirectness which follows from the way in which nevertheless he has to do with us. That God acts is a reality: it is the reality of his trustworthiness; but we do not see him directly. And even the way in which he acts is accessible to us only in terms of our faith in him. We cannot prove that he acts here, or here: we can only live in the faith that he does act.

Since the action of God is only accessible to us in this double indirectness, we may equally speak of what happens to us as the reality of God. When we speak of what happens to us, in the relation of faith, we are speaking of God's act. And when we speak of God's act we speak of what he is. The basic utterance of faith is that God is true: what he does to us is what he is.

But, it might be objected, can we not equally say that if we may speak of God only in what he does to us, we must abandon any talk of God as he is? Is the concept of God's being not unnecessary, indeed, strictly not deducible from his act? And if we cannot speak of God being, but only of God acting, have we not started on the slippery slope towards a mere anthropologizing of the whole experience of faith? Must we not, therefore, put a brake on the

[1]*Der Mensch zwischen Gott und Welt*, p. 228.

whole procedure, and insist that we start from and end with
the One-who-is?

Traditionally, theology has put on this brake, a brake
which it has borrowed from philosophy: God is the first
cause, *causa sui*, who lives *a se*, from himself, whose aseity is
the source of everything in the cosmos.

But so long as the being of God is conceived in terms of
substance, as a static entity, then it seems to me that we
are not helped. What we are then offered is an objective
entity, conceived of as somehow both alongside all other
entities in the cosmos, and at the same time above all other
entities, or, as Tillich would rather say, the ground of all
being. The basic flaw in this way of conceiving the being
of God is that it wishes simultaneously to have two contra-
dictory things: it wishes to have God as the source of all
that is, and it wishes to have God as a demonstrable and
objectively manageable phenomenon within all that is.[1]
This is a contradiction which staggers the reason. Its
underlying presupposition is that there are two worlds,
the world of phenomena, and the world in which God is,
or which God is. Once this dualism is posited, there is no
way of thinking the two worlds together again. This is
the theological form of the dualism which haunts western
philosophy, and which reached its logical extreme in
Averroes' theory of a double truth.

But it may be asked whether Christian faith can understand its situation in any other way. Is this not the paradox
of God's being, that though he is utterly different, and
infinitely distant in his difference, he is nevertheless utterly
one with us, and infinitely near? Can we really circumvent

[1] I do not imply that Paul Tillich conceives of God as an object among
objects. But the problem exists, and it is part of the grandeur of
Tillich's thought that he struggles honestly with it. See especially his
Biblical Religion and the Search for Ultimate Reality.

the traditional dualism which is expressed in such terms as 'transcendent' and 'immanent'?

Now it seems clear that if we hold by the qualitative difference of God from all that is in the cosmos, we are bound to hold by some kind of dualism. This means that we are bound to hold by some notion of transcendence. Without this, our faith could as easily be described as mere human self-expression. And without a God who is utterly other, we could say, indeed we should be bound to say, that God is just everything that happens to us. The way would then be open for all kinds of subjectivism, and if the idea of God were retained at all, it would be by simple identification of God with nature and history: in other words, pantheism. This was the basis of the kind of nationalism which was so sharply opposed by the Confessing Church in Germany during the Nazi régime, which saw in the *Blut und Boden*, the blood and soil, of the German people the revelation of God's purpose. God was then simply the expression of a natural and historical drive. Similarly in the Marxist theory, God, so far as he survives, is simply the summary for the monistic course of human history.

Therefore we cannot abandon the reality of transcendence without falling into entirely naturalistic and in the end solipsistic attitudes. Without the otherness which is expressed by the concept of transcendence we should end in the utter loneliness of the separated self.

But it is when we ask just how we experience this reality of transcendence that a way through our difficulty may be seen. The reality of transcendence is not properly comprehended in terms of a metaphysical postulating of substances, or of two worlds, or of two heterogeneous entities. But the reality of transcendence is experienced as an event which happens to us. We are confronted by the other. Here in time and space, in the midst of our temporal history, in our very historicity, and constituting that historicity, we are faced by the other. The reality of transcendence encounters us when we are aware of the presence of another centre of will and of personal being. It is the otherness of the human other, of the other I, the I who is a Thou to me, and to whom I in turn am a Thou, in mutuality of historical existence, which constitutes the actuality of transcendence. Transcendence is thus not a reality separate from us, but is the way in which we express the historical reality of encounter with others. Transcendence is not an entity with a separate being of its own, but is the way in which being is: namely, in relation with others. This relation is thus an action, not a state: it is the act or venture of mutual existence.

In an analogous way, we suggest, we may speak of the relation with God. His transcendence, too, is the expression for the historical reality of his encounter with his creatures. The way in which he is is therefore always *in actu*: it is a way of movement, a dynamic personal being-for-us. God's being is thus relational through and through.

So in this encounter with otherness, while we speak necessarily of dualism, of the one and the other, there is at the same time a fundamental monism: we are all bound up together in the one world, the world of relation. God's otherness is only expressible in terms of his historical being for us. So he cannot be as it were located outside space, nor can he be given an extra-temporal dimension from which we try somehow to think of him as emerging, in order to have to do with us in space and time. All that we can say of God is indissolubly bound up with what he is for us in space and time. God's historicity is the way in which we understand his transcendence and his immanence together: but the historicity is the concrete reality from which the transcendence and the immanence are abstractions.

In speaking thus of transcendence and immanence as abstractions from the concrete historicity of encounter we have deliberately discarded the speculative idealist approach. On this view you begin with two disparate entities, the finite and the infinite, or the positive objective world and an ideal super-world, and analyze the ways in which they may be understood as related, or even as flowing into one another. Starting from two incommensurable substances, you cannot but end in contradiction, or in the swallowing up of the one by the other. But if you start, as we have done, from the phenomenological world, from the actuality of our experience, then it is possible to speak of the encounter of human personal existence with other existences, and by analogy, with God.

Does this mean that we have to abandon the concept of sheer being, as we have abandoned the concept of sheer transcendence? Can we speak of being that lies beyond all that we experience in personal encounter? Here, it seems to me, we must again fall back into the trusting silence of negative theology. We cannot speak of God in himself. We cannot speak of God as he is. We cannot put any content into the concept of God's being. We can only speak in terms of the ways in which we actually encounter otherness. These terms are basically historical. And all that we can say of the absolutely Other, of God, is that in his paradoxical giving of himself to us, which we receive in faith, the faith that we are forgiven and reconciled, we do indeed believe that it is not simply of ourselves and of the human other that we are speaking, but of God. In every I-Thou relation we glimpse the eternal Thou.[1]

[1]Martin Buber, *I and Thou*, London, 1937, p. 6: 'In every sphere in its own way, through each process of becoming that is present to us, we look out toward the fringe of the eternal *Thou*; in each we are aware of a breath from the eternal *Thou*; in each *Thou* we address the eternal *Thou*.'

In the strength, then, of this faith, we must say that God includes time and history in himself. For all those who are in relation with him—and that means, for all that exists outside him—God is not anything else than temporal and historical. He does not abolish time, he does not destroy history. But he accepts them as the way of his being: being not as an ideal otherness, but being as being for others. The traditional word for this circumlocution, 'being for others', is love.

In terms of this traditional word, love, we may therefore summarize our understanding of transcendence as a temporal and historical experience of an actual encounter, in which the self is continually overcome, both judged and forgiven, and then renewed in being for others. It is in this being for others that the act of God is to be apprehended —not direct, not as a theophany or an objectifiable miracle, not comprehensible, not fully expressible—as the way of his love. We cannot get nearer to God than this: he is not accessible in isolation or in abstraction, as a being, or as being itself. He is known only as he gives himself, and in this giving he expresses himself as entirely historical.

'He that hath seen me hath seen the Father.'

7. The meaning of history

When we ask now the question of meaning in history, we do so more in order to clarify what we have already said than with any intention of adumbrating still another 'philosophy of history'.

Our basic question is not, What is the meaning of history? but, Is there any meaning in history at all? And the simple answer is: we cannot tell. But to this answer we must add, 'But we can give it a meaning.'

I remind you that I am asking a theological question, that is, a question which arises out of the relation to God in faith. There is a striking resemblance between the answer of theology and that of a sensitive humanist like Karl Popper, who writes, 'Although history has no meaning, we can give it a meaning.'[1] The difference, however, is twofold. First, we say that so far as human knowledge is concerned we do not have the whole of history available to our scrutiny, and so we cannot tell whether it may be meaningful. And second, the giving of meaning to history is not the mere consequence of our own resolution, but is a concomitant of eschatological faith.

If the question about meaning were asked outside this faith, then clearly it can be, and has been, answered in a multitude of ways. History has one meaning to a Marxist, another to Spengler, another to Toynbee, and so on. Each

[1] *The Open Society*, II, p. 278.

of these provides us with a philosophy of history, in terms of an ideology. But faith in its historical self-understanding refuses to be transposed into a philosophy of history or a world-view. From the standpoint of such philosophies we must conclude that history is thoroughly relativist. It is meaningful to this or that kind of philosopher in terms of his own particular presuppositions, prejudices, and hopes. So in this context we can certainly speak of meaning in history, but it is a plurality of conflicting meanings, and conflicting histories. And this plurality can extend across many civilizations, some overlapping, some isolated.

But even from within the relation of faith it is not possible to exclude this relativism. On the contrary, it is necessary to accept and understand it as integral to the meaning which we are enabled to give to history. For it is in its unpredictable, creative particularity that history can be given meaning, and this particularity implies thorough relativism.

'History is the field of human decisions.'[1] We may even say, history is what men decide in the light of their self-understanding. But this understanding cannot be identified with a clearly discernible progress towards some more or less clearly discernible goal. The teleological hypothesis is no more tenable here, amid the relativities and unpredictabilities of events, than it is in connexion with the so-called 'proof' of God's existence. For meaning in the sense of progress, or inevitable development, or the triumph of good, or the attainment of a classless society, or some other movement towards a vague goal or a clearly defined end, is merely a wilful imposition of an ideology upon the confused field of particular decisions.

This confusion is not resolved by a study of the story of Christendom. Are we to see a proof of the purposive devel-

[1]Rudolf Bultmann, '*Zum Problem der Entmythologisierung*', in *Kerygma und Mythos* IV, p. 21.

opment of history in the activities of the Spanish Inquisition? Or is the expansion of Christianity in the nineteenth and the first part of the twentieth centuries a proof of an over-all pattern to history? It might seem more plausible to accept Tertullian's epigram, that 'the blood of the martyrs is the seed of the church'. But this too can only be taken in the paradoxical terms of an eschatological faith, for there is no self-evident connexion between the destiny of the martyrs and any general theory of history.

The suffering of Christ, which was the content of his whole life, not just an accidental conclusion to his life, is the real stop which is set to all large generalizations about the meaning of history. And we may add that the countless individuals who have suffered, the great anonymous host of sufferers of torments at the hands of men, of injustice, of misery, of meaninglessness, of pain of body and agony of spirit, are a cloud of witnesses who point the finger of scorn upon all the neat and tidy optimisms which try to sweep all this accumulation of suffering under the carpet, and offer us a tidy scheme, like a well-ordered parish, where everything is cheerful and brittle.

No philosophy of history, as the attempt to impose an unconditioned meaning on the stream of the conditioned, is available to Christian faith. The philosophy of progress is not a Christian concept. We may indeed say that God who holds all his creation in the hollow of his hand sees a finished pattern, a total meaning. But this is just another way of saying that we *believe* in God's goodness and grace. If we are asked to explicate this belief, we are bound to be at a loss.

I have already discussed the defects of the fashionable view of *Heilsgeschichte*, the history of redemption or salvation history. I have discarded the attempt to point to objectively available moments in the course of history as proof of meaning in history. From the standpoint of philosophies of history in general, the *heilsgeschichtliche* view is just another attempt to select certain objective happenings. It is bound by all the rules of profane history, working by the usual presuppositions about cause and effect. It is like a ghostly imposition upon the rest of history, a selective spiritualizing of history which is in the last analysis dependent on the subjective whim of the 'Christian' historian. It is a denial of the existential historicity of the *Heilsgeschichte* of Christ to try to accommodate it to the terms of an objectifiable flow or development or progress of events.

Nevertheless, as I have said, while we cannot discern any pattern or purpose in what of history is available to us in general, but can only construct little histories of a limited kind, we are able to give history a meaning. We are able to do this in terms of our own particular and free decisions. 'The perception of the historical process is itself a historical event.'[1] The man who looks at the past is making a decision about that past, and about his own future. Man's authentic existence includes openness for the future, in a freedom which takes place again and again. So the meaning of history is given in the recurring moment in which a man freely decides concerning his future.

This possibility of free decision, and thus of giving meaning to history, arises in the confrontation with Christ as the eschatological event. Out of the events of the past there enters our present the word of judgment and of promise, summoning us to authentic existence. This means that though we cannot see the whole course of history, and thus are never able to speak of the meaning of history as a whole, we are able to place our life unreservedly into God's hands. Or, to leave the metaphor, and put the matter in terms of our actual temporality, we are enabled to accept history as

[1] Bultmann, *op. cit.*, p. 20.

meaningful, as coming out of a future which is God's and not our own.

It is in this context that we may speak of Providence. We may heartily agree with Professor McIntyre's general line of thought. Providence is bound up with the 'redemptive work of God in Jesus Christ', or, as I should put it, with the eschatological faith in Christ. Thus Providence is to be understood precisely in the terms of judgment and forgiveness which I have already put forward as the central elements in this faith. I find it more difficult to agree that these elements are part of 'the discernible pattern of Providence'. Is it really possible to speak of a discernible pattern? Can we really say that 'God's judgment is seen in the manner in which disaster finally overtakes those who deny the Sovereignty of God'? And is it possible to say that 'God's mercy . . . is seen in the fact that God so often gives time for repentance'? What of the fact that God so often does not give time for repentance? But it is fair to note that Professor McIntyre does recognize the serious problem of human freedom, which he rightly calls one of 'the profoundest paradoxes in the Christian faith'. And we must express our profound agreement with all that he has to say about the lack of empirical observable unity in history, and its fragmentariness, even in a sense for God as well as ourselves.[1]

But we should add that it can never be any different. The working out of the Providence of God is strictly tied to his act in Christ. Even the Pauline *locus classicus* for the Christian view of Providence—'And we know that all things work together for good to them that love God, to them who are the called according to his purpose'[2]—is an affirmation of faith, not of knowledge, in the sense of a theory about

[1]See John McIntyre, *The Christian Doctrine of History*, pp. 36*ff.*
[2]Romans 8.28.

the whole of history in its particularity. We may believe that God rules, and even that he overrules both individual and group purposes. But we cannot prove it, nor can we discern it. We may venture to speak of our faith in God's Providence solely in the reality of the end to all history, regarded as human effort, self-assertion and self-justification, which is acted out in the life and death of Christ, and in the reality of the new possibilities given in and through that judgment. But of the way of that Providence, the means by which God's will is accomplished, we cannot say more than we are already enabled to say in faith.

Admittedly, what we have to say might well incur the reproach of being so formalized that it looks like a mere assertion of faith empty of any content. We have still to discuss the question of the style of faith in a secular world. Meantime we must say that we may not venture beyond the realm of faith. We are not to expect to see the finger of God at work in this or that period or movement in history, any more at one point than at another. The truth by which faith holds is rather that at any point in history, that is, at any point in the life of the man of faith, there may arise the possibility of God's providential care, that is, his grace, by which the man is grasped and enabled to accept his destiny. But any generalized statement, objectifying this faith either by means of a philosophy of history, or a meta-history, or an empirical 'proof' of the working of Providence, comes to grief on the necessary reserve, even scepticism, with which, if we are realistic, we must face the riddles of history.

But one little step more out of our necessary reserve we are enabled to take, and it is decisive. We may affirm that God is related to history as a father to his son: not just that God acts in history, or in selected events of history, but that God exists for us in history—in all history, so far as that history is the reality of human existence. And history is the reality of human existence: it is that which man is in his authentic freedom. In a secondary sense history is that for which man is responsible. But the further significance of that responsibility will appear more plainly when we come to discuss the meaning of secularism.

III. SECULARISM

I. *Introduction*

'Man can never jump out of time, but has only to choose whether his present is determined by the past or the future.' These words from an early essay of Rudolf Bultmann's might be taken as the summary of the way we have so far gone. We have examined the peculiarity of faith as a way of existence, which is thoroughly historical both in its source and in its shape and style, being at one and the same time a free decision and an acknowledgment of utter dependence and receptivity. Then without detracting from the reality of the forgiving act of God, indeed in dependence upon it, I spoke of the responsible freedom in which the man of faith finds himself in relation to his world. Equally, when I came to talk specifically of history, I indicated that our attitude to the riddle of historical existence is not simple, but ambiguous. The difficult problem of defining what we mean by history reaches an acute point when we ask the kind of question which Kierkegaard asked so persistently that theology has never been the same since: the question how we are related for our eternal blessedness to events of the past, and especially to the life and death of Jesus.

I tried to answer that question in terms of a new understanding of eschatology. Christ is the end, the last one, the last Adam, as St Paul calls him: in him all history is both judged and forgiven. But this does not mean that henceforth the man of faith lives apart from the world. There is indeed an immense pull in Christian faith towards complete abnegation and renunciation of the world. St Paul expresses it when he says 'to depart and be with Christ is far better'.[1] But once again the matter is not simple, but ambiguous. For the Christian is not enjoined to commit suicide, for he is not enjoined simply to renounce the world. Rather, we have to understand a complex situation: the man of faith recognizes that all his life, its entire history, as a movement of self-assertion and self-justification in the world—what St Paul calls 'boasting'[2]—has been brought to its extreme limit in the judgment passed on it by the life and death of Christ. But simultaneously he recognizes that this judgment is the effective forgiveness and liberation from his past. Henceforth, therefore, he lives in a recurrent anticipation of the end. That is to say, the future, now acknowledged as God's future, is paradoxically present to the man of faith.

It is of the utmost significance that in this dialectical situation faith does not abolish or annul history. That is, the place and time of the man of faith remain what they have been since he entered space and time. He is not snatched up into heaven, he is not removed from time into eternity. Certainly, we are able to speak, and must speak, of God's act in Christ as coming really from God and not from the immanent possibilities of the world. It comes from beyond man's own possibilities. But it comes to man as thoroughly historical. In considering the way in which we understand how God acts we have said that this historicity is the very way in which God is. We cannot speak of God in terms of is-ness, in the sense of an objective state or a substance, but we can only speak of his being as a being for us in history.

But, we went on to say, this does not mean that God is

[1] Philippians 1.23.   [2] Romans 3.27.

to be identified with all that happens in history. He is not a God that becomes, an emergent God, of one piece with the ultimate meaning of the entire course of history, for example in the Hegelian sense in which there is a final synthesis of subjective and objective spirit in the absolute spirit. The notion of the progressive fulfilment of the god-ness of God in the unfolding of history is remote from the Christian understanding. Nevertheless, though we speak of God as transcendent, in the sense that he acts upon our lives beyond all that is possible to ourselves out of our own powers in this world, this transcendence is not and can never for us be anything else but his historicity, that is, his being for us in time and space. As Körner says, 'the act of God transcends history within history.'[1]

In this way the prime temptation of theology throughout the life of Christendom is kept at bay: I mean the temptation to think docetically, that is, to think of God in Christ as not taking this world and its history quite seriously, but rather as a solemn fiction, a setting in which the supernatural work of God in Christ is played out, with the ultimate intention of abstracting men from their unreal existence. Such a view strikes at the heart of Christian faith, which is always and only established in and through the eminent historicity of the existence of Christ. And through this faith, along with Christ, the whole world is reinstated by God.

In making this general affirmation, however, we have by no means reached a position which is adequate for facing our tasks and duties in the world in a responsible way. It is especially today that we have to ask ourselves just what the relation of Christian faith is to all the busy activities and enterprises of men. What is the meaning of it all? And has it any relation to Christian faith? Or, if we live by

[1]Johannes Körner, *Eschatologie und Historie*, p. 42.

faith, are we simply disinterested in all this? Are we
to regard it as merely neutral activity? Or again, is it to
be regarded as activity which is hostile to faith? As the
rebellious pride of man defying his Lord in novel
ways? Are the planned journeys to the moon just a variation on the building of the tower of Babel, and is the investigation of the sources of life just a new version of Adam's
sin?

One thing is clear. Over the whole world today there
extends an activity which, superficially at least, is independent of the considerations which have so far occupied our
interest. The tide of secularism has swept over the whole of
the western world, the world that was once called Christendom, and beyond that it has reached into every land. It has
penetrated the lands which were formerly isolated from
Europe in their cultural background, and has included them
all in its sweep. It has flooded over every island and the
remotest parts of the world.

The reactions from some of the alien cultures, for instance
from that of Buddhism, are not surprising. But these
reactions, with their complicated roots in nationalism, and
anti-colonialism, as well as in religion, will not, it seems to
me, be able to avert the general reduction of all modern
societies to the unitary level of secularism.

This is at any rate true of secularism in its obvious aspect.
This obvious aspect is one in which the technological dynamism of the West is able to produce effects of immense
material significance. Sometimes, indeed, it seems as
though the basic attraction of what the West has to offer
to the rest of the world consists in the provision of a vast
system of welfare: roads and air-lines, cement and diesel
engines, Coca-Cola and fertilizers. It is hard to criticize
a way of life by which in fact we all live. Yet the question
cannot help arising: what does it all mean? Where is it

all leading? I cannot help thinking of a remark of John Ruskin's, when he was informed by a friend that a cable had been laid across the bed of the Atlantic, so that now people in London could speak with people in New York. John Ruskin was not impressed. All he said was: 'Have they anything to say to one another?'

The fact is that in its superficial aspects the tide of secularism is tending to reduce everything to the same boring mediocrity and conformism, to one style and taste: to a life which basically does not emerge from the impersonal world of It, from the collective in which everything is alike because everyone thinks alike, and thinks, moreover, in clichés and slogans: a world which is well stocked with ready victims of demagogy and bigotry, of fanaticism and philistinism.

This is the price which is at present being paid for a truly unexampled surge forward in the means of production and even, to a limited extent, in the means of distribution. The question which we have now to face is whether this price needs to be paid: or whether there is not some better hope, and some better way.

The question of what we are to do now in the midst of this secular world in which all of us, whatever our official allegiance, party line, or faith, now live, can only be answered when we understand where this secular world has come from, and what its real possibilities are. Only then can we hope to be really responsible to the challenge of our time. It is to these questions of roots that we must now turn. And they will determine our understanding of what is to be done. What future is to determine our lives? The future of ever-deepening fear and mistrust, joined with ever more staggering achievements in the technical realm, which in the context of this fear can only be compared to the superhuman efforts of a hysterical—some would say, a possessed—person? Or a future of ever-expanding possibilities in a context of trust and love?

The hope for our time can only lie in a new assessment of the powers of secularism. And this new assessment depends in the first instance upon our understanding of its sources.

2. *The history of the term 'secular'*

Clearly the connexion I have already indicated between secularism and the immense technological advances of our time is no more than an end-product of an activity which reaches far back into our history. It is significant that this history is that of the western world. In whatever ways we may delimit the term 'western', at least we mean by it not the story of Asia or China or Africa, not even Byzantium, but the story of the European West. To what extent, then, and in what sense, is secularism connected with the Christianity which lies in the background of Europe? And to what extent, and in what sense, is it in conflict with, or indifferent to, that Christian background?

In order to attempt answers to these and similar questions it is necessary to uncover, as far as possible, the sources of modern secularism. This I propose to do in two parallel analyses, first by an examination of the history of the word itself, and second by a theological examination of the concept.

The word *saeculum*, of uncertain origin, is regularly found in classical Latin to mean 'generation', 'age', 'long period of time.' The so-called 'secular' games of antiquity were so described because they were held at long but regularly recurring intervals. In Christian usage *saeculum* came to mean the world as opposed to the church, and is equivalent in Augustine with *mundus*, world. Similarly in English we find as early as 1290 the attested usage of 'secular' meaning belonging to the world, as distinct from the church and religion; civil, lay, temporal, chiefly with the negative sense of 'non-ecclesiastical, non-religious, or non-sacred'.[1]   A secondary usage denoted the clergy who did not live in an order but in the world as 'secular'. In Hooker's *Ecclesiastical Polity*, 1597, we find a typical example in the following: 'Religion and the fear of God as well induceth secular prosperitie as everlasting blisse in the world to come.' This well-defined neutral usage persisted into the nineteenth century.

But a new quality was added to the word by the actualities of European history. It was at the discussions which led to the Peace of Westphalia, in 1646, that the word *séculariser* was used by the French plenipotentiary as being acceptable, or at least tactful, in relation to the ecclesiastical and legal presuppositions of the treating parties. In this context, indeed, it meant the expropriation of ecclesiastical property for worldly purposes; but the hard truth was veiled by the terminology. In the eighteenth century the veil was lifted, and secularization in this specific sense was argued to be the rational and natural order of things which required to be restored. By the end of the century the very existence of 'spiritual princedoms' was being questioned—and that by the ecclesiastical authorities themselves. Thus the cathedral chapter of Fulda set a prize essay in 1785 with the theme, 'What are the defects of the spiritual states and how are they to be removed?' Mortmain was unable to withstand the general and growing sense of the fittingness of ever more secularization.

The great secularization consequent upon the French Revolution was thus no more than a step, if a large one, in a steady progression. The declaration of the French National Assembly, made at the instigation of Talleyrand, may be

[1]*Oxford English Dictionary, s.v.*

taken as a convenient summary of a process which had, indeed, been present in fact if not in name since the Vandals overran North Africa: '*Tous les biens ecclésiastiques sont à la disposition de la nation.*' However, it would be misleading to include all earlier acts of expropriation, especially those at the time of the Reformation, under precisely the same term. Or at least we must exclude any polemical connotation from those earlier acts of 'secularization', since the intention of the Reformers was to re-vivify the union rather than to accentuate the difference between spiritual and worldly interests. As Stallmann points out, 'As a political concept secularization is characteristic of the age in which political power became an independent worldly power, and in which at the same time religion was increasingly distinguished as the "inward" affair of man from his "outward", political and civil status.'[1]

It was in England that the next significant development of the word took place. The Oxford English Dictionary dates the following definition in 1851: 'The doctrine that morality should be based on regard to the well-being of mankind in the present life, to the exclusion of all considerations drawn from belief in God or a future state.'

The definition presumably derives from one of the many writings of George Jacob Holyoake. His views, in spite of their nineteenth-century colouring (perhaps to some extent because of it), are prophetic of so much that is accepted almost without reflection in our own time, and not only by professed secularists, that we propose to give a short account of one of his publications.

Holyoake lived from 1817 to 1906. He was early attracted to the views and ideals of Robert Owen, and became a lecturer in the Owenite movement. In 1841 he had the unenviable distinction of being the last person to be jailed

[1]Martin Stallmann, *Was ist Säkularisierung?*, p. 12.

in England for public blasphemy, and served a sentence of six months in Gloucester jail. It may in fact have been this experience which led him to coin the more innocuous term 'secularism', in preference to 'atheism', to describe his position. He was a busy editor and writer, and towards the end of his long life he published a two-volume autobiography.

One of the freshest and most vigorous accounts of his views may be found in a volume entitled *Christianity and Secularism*, published in London in 1863. This volume contains the verbatim report of a public discussion which took place in January and February of that year between Holyoake and an Independent minister. The general question to which the speakers addressed themselves was 'What advantages would accrue to mankind generally, and the working classes in particular, by the removal of Christianity, and the substitution of secularism in its place?'

While it is impossible to avoid having a certain sympathy for Holyoake's opponent, so clearly inferior in the practice of such debates, this sympathy is in the end wasted. For the clerical disputant just as clearly belongs to that class whom David Hume described as 'furious Christians'. Holyoake, on the other hand, was an accomplished controversialist, with an intense moral concern. Indeed, he is so serious, so high-minded, and so persistent that he must sometimes, surely, have given ever so slight an impression to his associates that he was a bore.

He disclaims any ambition to be a system-builder, principally because the working classes whom he wishes to serve are 'bewildered already by arbitrary systems, and exhausted by the struggles to live.' What he offers is 'simple directions and practical guidance'.[1] Here he stands squarely in the empirical tradition of Bentham and John Stuart Mill. He

[1] *op. cit.*, p. 5.

puts his presuppositions as follows: 'We believe in relative Truth and discretionary Silence; in Reason as a test; in Science as a power; in Service as a duty; and in Endurance as a virtue.'[1] As to the existence of God he is simply agnostic. Morality he defines as 'that system of human duties commencing from man',[2] which is distinct from religion, 'that system of human duties assumed to commence from God'.[3]

He defines a secularist as 'one who gives primary attention to those subjects the issues of which can be tested by the experience of this life. The secularist principle requires that precedence should be given to the duties of this life over those which pertain to another world.'[4] Although for the purposes of the debate he insists that he is only claiming *precedence* for the concerns of this life, it is clear from the course of the debate itself that these concerns in practice exclude and render unnecessary any other-worldly theistic system. His story of the old professors of 'abstract theology', that 'one is milking the barren heifer, and the others are holding the sieve',[5] makes his attitude sufficiently clear. But, as he adds, 'you cannot reform the world by a logical *coup d'état*. You must be content to study men in groups, and meet their states of thought specially and patiently.'[6]

The weight of his argument is that attention to temporal things is based upon practical experience of 'the living interests of the hour',[7] whereas Christianity is a matter of speculation. The Christianity he wishes to displace is defined as 'moulding human duties to suit the prospects of another life'.[8] Philosophical distinctions, however, are not really in his line. He is more at home with practical recommendations. Thus about the use of the Sabbath he writes, 'The precept, "Keep the Sabbath-day holy", we would interpret into keeping it healthfully, usefully, instructively.

[1] p. 6.   [2] p. 7.   [3] p. 7.   [4] p.8.   [5] p. 8.   [6] p. 9.
[7] p. 6.   [8] p. 22.

Secularism would take, when necessary, the poor factory-jaded Sunday scholars into fields—that schoolroom of nature! It would throw open the Clyde on the Sunday to the Sunday steamer, that the poor Glasgow weaver might gaze on Ben Lomond on the Lord's day. It would give the mechanic access to museums, and botanical gardens, crystal palaces, and even to the theatre on that day. We would do it, because one drama of Shakespere is a nobler creation than any sermon which was ever preached . . .'[1]

In brief, Holyoake wishes to 'free the Secular sphere . . . to authorize all men to walk in it without alarm of any kind, like that created by . . . many parts of the New Testament . . . We should not pray for the people, after the Church and Dissenting manner—we should seek to help them. We should not send dogma missionaries to the heathen—we should send arts, sciences, and instructors.'[2] 'Leave religious dreamers to wait on supernatural aid—let us look to what man can do for man.'[3] Thus 'it is in vain that the miner descends into the earth with a prayer on his lips unless he carries . . . a Davy lamp in his hand.'[4] 'During the prevalence of a pestilence an hospital is more value than a college of theologians.'[5] Against the doctrine of 'special interposition' Holyoake boldly sets the world of man, guided by what scientific powers he is able to acquire. And we have a good insight into his compassion and practical bent in the reference to 'the first sad view of life which breaks in upon the working man, whether he be a white slave or a black one,' in which 'might is God and Poverty is fettered.' 'Every stick and stone, every blade of grass, every bird and flower, every penniless man, woman, and child, has an owner in this England of ours no less than in New Orleans.'[6]

[1] *op. cit.*, p. 20.   [2] p. 39*f*.   [3] p. 40.   [4] p. 64.   [5] p. 64.
[6] p. 66.

I have given such extensive quotations from Holyoake's views because it is these views which, by and large, represent the common attitude of modern secular man. Holyoake has triumphed over his opponent all along the line. And even the theology has changed in our time.

One last quotation summarizes Holyoake's views:

The problem solved by secularism is this, that this partially comprehended and unexplored universe is yet, in its material and ascertainable relations to man, a possible theatre of the limitless happiness of humanity —that the light of duty may be seen, that a life of usefulness may be led, indefinite refinement may be attained, and tranquillity in death, and the highest desert in untried existence beyond us may be won, though the Origin of all things shall be hidden from us, and the Revelations of every religious sect shall be rejected.[1]

We may leave the debate between the ill-assorted opponents with one quotation from Holyoake's opponent: 'It [the bible] comes to rule this life, not to regulate the next—it lays down no hereafter duties. All the duties of Christianity are now on earth—deeds done in the body, or, if you will so call them, secular duties.'[2]

With this concession, and this definition, a new evaluation of the secular is made possible. But before we take up this possibility, it is helpful to see how the history of the term 'secular' has fared in even more recent times.

In brief, it has retained the firm connexion given to it by Holyoake with a positivist view of society, and a pragmatic and empirical view of life. A typical illustration of the state of affairs almost till our own day is the report of the world conference of the International Missionary Council, held in Jerusalem in 1928. There is an embarrassment and vagueness in dealing with the chosen theme of secularism, which

[1] pp. 221ff.   [2] p. 34.

are unfortunately still typical of the official church attitude today. The embarrassment can be ascribed to the fact that the practical manifestations of secularism are on the whole not openly or violently opposed to the interests of the churches or of Christianity, but are neutral, even indifferent, to these interests. For the realm in which Christianity is supposed to be active, namely, that of the 'other-worldly', is simply irrelevant to secularist activity. The vagueness, even contradictions, in the Christian attitude are less easily explained. It was characteristic of the Jerusalem conference that one speaker should find it possible to say that 'we are agreed on the fact of the opposition of secular civilization to Christianity',[1] and that on the very next page of the report another speaker should say that 'in many of its aspects secular civilization is a disinterested pursuit of human welfare.'[2]

A more forward-looking view was expressed by Canon Charles Raven, who said:

It will be necessary for us to accept all this rich contribution of this new way of life (secularism) . . . Secular civilization has provided a satisfying opportunity for personal development, not only in the pursuit of truth, but also in the providing of outlets for activities which supply all the values which religion was accustomed to provide . . . Our problem is to find how Christianity can baptize the new learning and the new social order with the spirit of Christ . . .[3]

We shall have to return to Raven's suggestion. Here we note that the main weight of opinion is expressed in the

[1]The Jerusalem Meeting of the International Missionary Council, 1928, I, p. 337.
[2]ibid., p. 338.
[3]ibid., p. 340f. I cannot help asking what Raven would say if the new learning and the new social order did not want to be 'baptized'.

leading paper by Rufus M. Jones on 'Secular Civilisation and the Christian Task', in which secularism, defined as 'a way of life and an interpretation of life that include only the natural order of things and that do not find God, or a realm of spiritual reality, essential for life and thought',[1] is regarded throughout quite undialectically as 'this vast unconquered rival',[2] and as 'a rival movement as powerful, as dangerous, as insidious as any of the great historical religions'.[3] Even the weightier reflections of Archbishop William Temple, which include his well-known description of Christianity as 'the most materialist'[4] of all religions, while their instinct is right, in their positive evaluation of secularism, depend for their cogency upon the unhappy identification of Christianity with progress.

An understanding of Christianity as pre-eminently historical demands a closer scrutiny of the real sources of modern secularism, and an appreciation of its further possibilities beyond the mere extension and proliferation of technological achievements. For these we must examine the historical powers inherent in Christianity itself.

---

[1] *ibid.*, p. 230.   [2] p. 232.   [3] p. 238.
[4] This is more fully worked out in Temple's Gifford Lectures, *Nature, Man and God*, p. 478.

3. *The source of secularism*

My thesis, put briefly, is that the source of secularism is to be found in Christian faith. Further, the relation of secularism to this faith is of such a kind that it cannot be simply noted as a historical fact of a merely genetical order. The relation continues into our time, and thus offers a historical hope to the present *malaise* of secularism. If this relation were not real, and capable of being further activated, the *malaise* could not be cured, and we should be left without hope.

There is a growing awareness today—chiefly, but not solely, among theologians—of the significance of this theme, the relation of secularism to faith. The contribution of Dietrich Bonhoeffer will be discussed when we come to consider the relation of religion to faith. Just because what he had to say is fragmentary and ambiguous it has perhaps been more effective than more straightforward work in spreading abroad a profound sense of disturbance with the traditional reactions of theology to 'worldly' hostility or indifference to the Christian message. The consultation on 'The Meaning of the Secular', held at the Ecumenical Institute at Bossey in Switzerland in 1959, marks a turning-point in the official Protestant and Orthodox view.[1] The

[1]The mimeographed papers read at this consultation are, I understand, obtainable from Bossey, as well as from the chairman, Dr Charles West, at Princeton Theological Seminary. My own paper there, on 'A

positive side of Rudolf Bultmann's hermeneutical work has always implied this interest. It comes out explicitly in one of his recent essays '*Der Gottesgedanke und der moderne Mensch*'.[1] I myself broached the theme in my earlier work *The New Man* (1956). One notable forerunner, in another field of enquiry, was Michael Foster. His three remarkable essays, published in *Mind* in October 1934, October 1935 and January 1936, on 'The Christian Doctrine of Creation and the Rise of Modern Natural Science', and 'Christian Theology and Modern Science of Nature', are a highly sophisticated presentation of the essential difference between the Greek (Platonic and Aristotelian) view of God and the world, and the Christian view. It is solely, he argues, on the basis of the Christian doctrine of creation that modern science was able to be established. What Foster has to say in terms of the scientific world-view and a doctrine of creation I am now attempting to say, *mutatis mutandis*, of the whole structure of modern society in relation to faith. Perhaps the most striking recent work is *Christianity and World History* (1964) by A. van Leeuwen, which is essentially concerned with the nature of the Christian mission today in the context of the world religions.

But the writer who has made the most elaborate and direct contribution to our theme is Friedrich Gogarten. It will be clear from what I have already noted that he is neither

---

Theological Perspective of the Secular', was reprinted in *The Christian Scholar*, March 1960. A forthcoming series of volumes on Church and Society, sponsored by the World Council of Churches, will certainly deal with the theme.

[1]This essay has appeared in *Zeitschrift für Theologie und Kirche*, December 1963, and an English translation will be found in a symposium on Bonhoeffer's thought, which I have edited, *World Come of Age* (to be published London, 1966).

solitary nor eccentric. And if I may venture a prediction, the immediate future of theology will be devoted to the problem of secularism.

One work of Gogarten's in particular, *Verhängnis und Hoffnung der Neuzeit* (1953), with its sub-title *Säkularisierung als theologisches Problem*—'Secularizing as a theological problem'—is devoted to a rigorous analysis of the meaning of faith in its relation both to God and to the world.

Let us look at the broad outlines of Gogarten's argument. These are not easy to reproduce, since the argument is closely packed, even dense, and a survey of it is bound to lose some of the force which arises from its carefully qualified and even circumscribed nature. And there is a tendency to rely so heavily on the understanding of the Christian kerygma as found in the teaching of Paul that a certain loosening and widening of the problem must be attempted beyond what Gogarten has done.

Essentially, Gogarten says, Christian faith frees man from the world. By the 'world' he means the cosmos or orderly world, as an enclosed and enclosing entity, of the Greeks. But he also means the divine principalities and powers which determine the life of pre-christian man. Faith frees man from the law of these 'elements', so far, that is to say. as they in fact enclose man and shut him off from his true state as a creature. The Christian is no longer separated by any of these powers, not even by death itself, from God.[1] From the point of view of the pious heathen, therefore, the Christians are rightly described as godless, as atheists. But, as we learn in the teaching of Paul, submission to these 'elements' is at best a state of tutelage from which Christ has set men free. Thus in Galatians 4.9*f.* we read:

Formerly, when you did not know God, you were in bondage to beings that by nature are no gods; but now

[1]Romans 8.38*f.*

that you have come to know God, or rather to be known by God, how can you turn back to the weak and beggarly elemental spirits, whose slaves you want to be once more?[1]

However, these powers are not essentially evil, or hostile to God. It is man's own sin which has made them so, by his deciding for 'this world' against God, worshipping and serving the creature rather than the Creator.[2] Now in being set free by faith for God as his Creator, man is simultaneously set free from the world. But he is not taken out of the world, rather, he is now lord over the world, and responsible for it: he becomes fellow-heir with Christ,[3] he is now son and heir.[4] He is henceforth responsible for his own history. In faith, therefore, the world belongs to him.

This is the meaning of the 'de-divinization' of the world, the dethroning of all the gods and powers of the world, which for Gogarten is the way in which faith works. Thus we may say that secularization is the historical working-out of the power of justification by faith, and is present from the beginning in the liberation of the Christian from the world for God. This liberation from the world for God means at the same time responsibility for the world. 'Secularizing has to do with the furthering of the freeing of man from the world, and of his lordship over it which is a consequence of the freedom, acquired in faith, of the son for the Father, through which the mythical world is replaced by the historical world.'[5]

This basic shift in the position of man does not mean, however, that from the time when faith became a historical possibility there were established principles and guiding lines for the transaction of the business of faith. Rather, there is a real liberation of the world and a real responsibility

[1]Cf. Colossians 2.8, 20f.   [2]Romans 1.24.   [3]Romans 8.17.
[4]Galatians 4.7.   [5]Gogarten, op. cit., p. 99.

of faith for the world. Thus we have the paradoxical situation that while the life of the son (that is, of the believer, who is able to call God Abba, Father) is nothing without the Father, at the same time the life of the son is also something for itself. There is a real autonomy, which is grounded in man's reason; and it is the very interest of faith that this autonomy of reason should be furthered. What faith, then, does in and for the world is to let the world be itself: with the aid of reason the man of faith gives expression to his historical responsibility. In fact, 'faith only exists where there is a secular relation of the believer to the world.'[1]

Christian faith is able to remain authentic only so long as it maintains this balance between its real historical freedom and its equally real dependence upon the Creator. Faith sees the world in its limits, in a 'questioning ignorance'.[2] If this questioning ignorance is abandoned over against the wholeness of the world, then this central concept of the whole is transformed into that of a 'closed whole'. And with this transformation we face the basic problematic nature of modern secularism. But faith does not try to solve this problem by providing an over-all answer to the question of human existence and history. To attempt this would mean to fall back into the state of being surrounded by the world, and becoming a part of the world, as a closed whole, once more. It is in this situation that modern secularism finds itself, so that its only way forward is by the manipulation of a future which it has already anticipated. From this manipulation there flow the various utopias and ideologies of modern times—or else nihilism. For if man attempts to anticipate his future in such ways, the only wholeness which he can realize is that of a world in which he is enclosed. Basically, in this attempt, man 'escapes from history and its futurity which simply cannot be anticipated'.[3]

[1]*op. cit.*, p. 141.　　　[2]p. 143.　　　[3]*op. cit.*, p. 201.

Or we may say that in this attempt man wishes to exchange faith for sight. He wishes to possess his future. But it is only by remaining in the responsible historicity, without foresight, which is given by and in faith that man can at the same time carry forward the authentic secularization of the world. Only in this way does the world remain man's world. In the attempt to escape from the situation of questioning ignorance man in fact becomes the world's, that is, a slave once more.

The grand merit of this analysis by Gogarten of the relation of faith to God and the world is its re-pristination of the Pauline teaching of justification by faith. He understands the reality of faith, therefore, to be not merely the genetic explanation of modern secularism, but also to be the intrinsic element in modern secularism without which this secularism cannot even understand itself for what it is; and without which it is bound to become a prey to its own ideologies.

At the same time it is necessary, it seems to me, to extend the historical grounding of this view of faith in its relation to God and the world. It should not be simply taken as a piece of Pauline teaching which has been put into modern terminology, and thus interpreted for our time. Presumably Gogarten himself would recognize the justice of this comment, since Paul's teaching is itself based upon the kerygma or message concerning Christ. This kerygma calls for faith in 'the Word made flesh'. In the terminology we have been using here this means that in Christ history is both man's history and God's history. It is in this history that an end is made to history conceived as a self-contained entity (Gogarten's 'closed whole'). It is in faith in Christ that the world is recognized as being cleared of gods and powers. It is in his actual historical being for the world that every possible meaning of the world in and for itself is cancelled.

This is signalized in the cry of dereliction from the Cross; for in this cry the world is even cleared of God: and only in this way is the world freed to become what it can become, namely, what God wishes it to be. The de-divinization of the world is thus complete in Christ. Certainly, we must add, as Gogarten has stressed, that it is faith that acknowledges this. It is faith that recognizes in Christ the absence of God. It is faith that recognizes that only in this way is any advent of God in Christ possible to man. Only in the sober and unmagical depths of that dereliction does historical life for man become possible. Thus in Christ the presence of God is dialectically conjoined with his absence. Thus we may recognize Christ as the truly secular man, the one who lives entirely by faith, and thus entirely freely for the world, and entirely freely for God.

So the kerygma summons us to faith in Christ as the historical event in which man's existence and God's existence are at one. It need hardly be said that by thus indicating the dynamic movement from the kerygma to faith, we do not mean to displace faith by an objective observation about the historical person of Jesus. We make no claim to be able to enter into the self-understanding of the historical Jesus. We do not consider it either possible or necessary to construct a portrait of the historical Jesus, or a speculation about the nature of his self-consciousness. What we have is the eschatological message concerning him, that, and nothing more.

It is in faith in the kerygma concerning Christ, therefore, that the possibility has been established for man to go his own way in a liberated world.

4. *The ambiguity of secularism*

In our theological analysis we have suggested that it is in the liberation of man which is brought about by faith that the source of secularism is to be found. Faith frees man from the world, and at the same time it frees him for the world in historical responsibility. Henceforth man is able to make his own history, 'because the creation itself will be set free from its bondage to decay and obtain the glorious liberty of the children of God.'[1] Faith then understands itself as being without any resting-place either within or outside of itself: neither in interior self-assertion and 'religious' feelings, nor in any view of a visible and ordered progression in the world outside. The significance of this essential restlessness of faith, as Kierkegaard called it,[2] of this 'holy hypochondria', as Hamann called it,[3] will have to be elaborated later, when we face the meaning of the collision in Christendom between faith and religion.

Meantime, however, we must follow up the hints we have already given concerning the ambiguity of the modern secularist position. Our theological analysis and the view which was so clearly expressed by Holyoake seem to be in

[1]Romans 8.21.
[2]See, e.g., his journal entry XI² A 29 (p. 195 of my edition of his journals, *The Last Years*, London, 1965).
[3]In a letter to Herder, 3rd June 1781. See my *J. G. Hamann*, London, 1960, p. 49.

flat contradiction with one another. As Karl Löwith has said, our world is 'Christian in origin and at the same time anti-Christian in result'.[1] Or as Holyoake, and many present-day secularists, would rather say, our world is simply indifferent to its Christian sources.

In other words, the modern secularist may be ready to recognize the source of his views, so far as the history of ideas is concerned, in Christian history. He may be ready to admit that ideas, knowledge and experience which are now capable of autonomous existence were originally part of a specifically Christian view of life. But just because they are capable of autonomy, the manner in which they reached this position no longer seems of great significance to him. On the whole the secularist of today has learned to regard the origin of his autonomy in a more limited historical perspective than that which we have indicated. He does not see it as stretching back to the biblical faith, and as intrinsic to the dynamism of faith at all. It is probably the fact that the typical modern secularist sees the emergence of his autonomy in a more polemical context, as arising out of the previous heteronomy. That is, he has noted the historical emergence, at the end of the middle ages of European history, of a view of man's life which rejected and threw off the bonds of a specific metaphysic, which purported to express, within the historical *corpus christianum*, the truth about man's life. This metaphysic allowed room for a doctrine of revelation and of grace which taught that man's life was completed by the superimposition of divine powers upon his natural existence. There was thus presupposed a cleavage between the natural and the supernatural spheres, and between the sacred and the profane.

With the rejection of this metaphysic there went a slow but steady rejection, covering in turn every activity of man's

[1] *Weltgeschichte und Weltgeschehen*, pp. 183*f.*

spirit, of the realities which this metaphysic attempted to represent. Today we have reached the point at which the straightforward secularist finds the 'God-hypothesis' simply irrelevant. But more, with the relinquishment of any need to hold on to a realm of 'supernature', there has also gone the loss of any felt sense of transcendence. Thus the fashionable talk about 'the death of God' includes two distinct elements. There is first the rejection of a specific metaphysic, and the idea of God which was elaborated in its terms. But secondly, the point is reached where God, and not just an idea of God, has simply dropped out. It is not that there is 'a God-shaped blank' in the life and the thought of those who deny him: there is no blank, God is undialectically absent: he is not. This is the death of God.

The earliest modern analysis of the first element in this movement, that is, the reflective rejection of a specific metaphysic, and the dogmatic theology which is its expression, is to be found in an early essay by Hegel, published in 1802, on *Glauben und Wissen*, 'Faith and Knowledge', with the sub-title 'or the Philosophy of Reflexion of Subjectivity, in the Perfection of its forms as Kantian, Jacobian and Fichtian Philosophy'.[1] I shall not attempt to analyze Hegel's critique of the three philosophers he discusses, beyond noting that he regards all three as having reached a similar negative position with regard to the possibilities of reason: the absolute is above reason, and thus the philosophers of Enlightenment are talking about 'an infinitely empty space of knowing'[2] which is only filled by the subjectivity of their

---

[1]Hegel, *Sämtliche Werke*, Jubiläumsausgabe, 1927, pp. 277–433. I owe the general reference to a note in the essay by Bultmann, already mentioned, 'Der Gottesgedanke und der moderne Mensch', *Zeitschrift für Theologie und Kirche*, December 1963, p. 336. The precise reference I owe to Professor William Maclagan.

[2]*loc. cit.*, p. 281.

empirical experience. Hegel's conclusion is what is of special interest to us here, and I attempt a translation of the cryptic sentences:

The pure concept, however, or infinity as the abyss of the *nihil* into which all being sinks, must characterize the infinite pain, which hitherto had historical existence only in culture and as the feeling on which modern religion rests—the feeling that God himself is dead (which was as it were only empirically expressed in Pascal's words, *la nature est telle qu'elle marque partout un Dieu perdu, et dans l'homme et hors de l'homme*)—purely as a moment, but no more than a moment, of the supreme idea. The pure concept must therefore give a philosophical existence to what was either a moral prescription of a sacrifice of empirical being or the concept of formal abstraction. Thus it restores to philosophy the idea of absolute freedom, and hence absolute suffering or a speculative Good Friday, which otherwise was historical, in the entire truth and hardness of its godlessness. And out of this hardness alone (since the serene element, the more unfathomable and individual element of the dogmatic philosophies as well as of the natural religions had to vanish) the supreme totality in all its seriousness can and must arise again from its deepest ground, all-embracing, into the serenest freedom of its form.[1]

So Hegel, recognizing the end of 'dogmatic philosophies', envisages a 'resurrection' of the 'supreme totality' in 'serenest freedom'. In Hegel this was not identical with atheism, though his methodical procedure, when separated from his all-embracing absolute spirit as well as from the particular historicity of the 'moment', leads quite easily to an undialectical atheism.

[1] *op. cit.*, p. 433.

It is the other element, not speculative and procedural, but experiential and even visionary, which supplies the powerful impetus beyond the thought of the death of God to the experience of nothing, to nihilism. The most shattering expression of this nihilism is to be found in a novel by Jean Paul, *Siebenkäs*, which appeared in 1796/7.[1] Jean Paul, one of the early 'romantic' writers in Germany, interrupts his story to recount the 'Speech of the dead Christ from the top of the structure of the universe, that there is no God'. In the preface to this speech Jean Paul speaks of how 'no one is so much alone in the universe as one who denies God—he mourns with an orphaned heart which has lost the supreme Father . . .' and then he launches upon his terrible vision of the church where the dead are stirring:

Now a tall and noble form, in pain without surcease, sank down from the heights on to the altar, and all the dead cried: 'Christ! Is there no God?'

He answered, 'None.'

The whole shadow of all the dead shook, not just the breast alone, and one after the other was torn by the shuddering.

Christ went on: 'I went through the worlds, I ascended into the suns, and flew along the milky ways through the wastes of heaven. But there is no God. I went down as far as being casts its shadow, and looked into the abyss, and called, "Father, where art Thou?" But I heard only the eternal storm, ungoverned, and the trembling rainbow of life stood without a sun that created it, and fell drop by drop into the abyss. And when I looked up to the immeasurable world for the divine eye, it glared at me with an empty and baseless socket; and eternity lay upon chaos and gnawed it and

[1]This reference too I owe to Rudolf Bultmann, *loc. cit.*, p. 335 *f.*

chewed the cud.—Cry on, discords, tear the shades apart with your crying. For He is not!'

[Then came the children and said] 'Jesus! Have we no father?' And he replied with streaming tears, 'We are all orphans, I and you, we have no father.'

Then the discords shrieked more violently—the trembling walls of the temple broke apart—the temple and the children sank down—and the whole earth and the sun sank after them—and the whole structure of the world sank past us, in its immeasurable extent—and at the summit of immeasurable nature Christ stood and gazed down into the structure of the world shattered by the light of a thousand suns, as it were into the pit hurled into eternal night, where the suns move like miners' lamps, and the milky ways like veins of silver.

. . . then tall as the supreme finite one he raised up his eyes to the void and to the unfathomable emptiness and said: 'Stiff and silent void! Cold and eternal necessity! Mad chance! Do you know it, among yourselves? When will you smash the whole structure, and me? . . . How alone each is in the broad tomb of the universe! I am only by myself. O Father, O Father, where is your infinite breast that I may rest upon it?— Alas, if each I is its own father and creator, why can it not also be its own destroying angel?'

. . . Here Christ looked down, and his eyes were filled with tears, and he said, 'Alas, once I lived upon the earth. Then I was still happy, then I still had my infinite Father, and still looked joyfully from the mountains into the infinite heaven, and pressed my pierced breast on its assuaging image, and still said in bitter death: "Father, draw your son out of the bleeding body and raise him to your heart!" Alas, you happy earth-dwellers, you still believe in him . . . you wretched ones, after death, your wounds will not be closed. When the wretched one lays himself down in the earth, with wounded back, to sleep into a more beautiful day, full of truth and joy and virtue, he awakes in tumultuous chaos, in eternal midnight, and no morning comes, and no healing hand, and no infinite father!—You mortal beside me, if you still pray, then pray to him: otherwise you have lost him for ever.'

And as I fell down and looked into the bright structure of the world I saw the rings of the great snake of eternity rising up around the universe, and falling down to coil yet again round the All, then winding a thousand times around nature, and squeezing the worlds together, crushing the infinite temple into one little church—and everything became narrow and dark and fearful—and an infinitely extended bell-clapper was about to sound time's last hour and shatter the structure of the universe —when I awoke.

My soul wept with joy that it could once more worship God—and my joy and weeping and faith in him were my prayer. And as I stood up, the sun gleamed deep behind the full purple ears of corn, and peacefully cast the reflection of its evening red upon the little moon, which rose without an aurora in the morning; and between heaven and earth a joyful and passing world stretched out its brief wings and lived, as I did, in face of the infinite Father. And from the whole of nature round about me there flowed out peaceful sounds, as from distant evening bells.[1]

This fearful vision is probably less well known to English readers than Nietzsche's story of the madman in *Fröhliche Wissenschaft*. With his cruder sensibility but subtler intellect

[1]Jean Paul, *Siebenkäs*, 'The Speech of the Dead Christ', after Part II, chapter 8.

he has made more impact on the modern consciousness. I give his story in full:

Have you not heard of the madman who lit a lantern at noonday, ran to the market-place, and cried unceasingly, 'I am looking for God! I am looking for God!' Since there happened to be many standing there who did not believe in God, he roused great laughter. 'Is he lost?' said one. 'Or gone astray like a child?' said another. 'Or has he hidden himself? Is he afraid of us? Has he gone on a voyage? Or emigrated?' So they shouted and laughed. The madman leapt into their midst, and pierced them with his glance. 'Where has God gone?' he cried. 'I will tell you. *We have slain him*—you and I. We are all his murderers. But how did we do it? How could we drink up the sea? Who gave us the sponge to wipe out the whole horizon? What did we do, when we unchained this earth from its sun? Where is it moving to now? And where are we moving to now? Away from all suns? Backwards, sideways, forwards, in every direction? Is there an above and a below any more? Are we not wandering as through infinite nothingness? Does empty space not breathe upon us now? Is it not colder now? Is not night coming, and ever more night? Must we not light lanterns at noon? Do we not hear the noise of the grave-diggers, as they bury God? Do we not smell God decaying?—Gods too decay! God is dead. God stays dead. And we have slain him. How shall we console ourselves, chief of all murderers? The holiest and most powerful that the world has ever possessed has ebbed its blood away beneath our knives —who will wipe this blood from our fingers? What water can make us clean? What propitiations and sacred rites will we have to invent? Is not the greatness of this deed too great for us? Must we not ourselves become gods, in order to seem worthy of it? There was never a greater deed, and because of it all who are born after us are part of a higher history than ever was before!'

The madman fell silent, and I looked at his hearers again. They too were silent, and looked at him with shocked eyes. At last he threw his lantern on the ground, so that it broke in pieces, and went out. 'I come too early,' he said, 'it is not yet my time. This monstrous event is still on the way—it has not yet penetrated men's ears. Lightning and thunder need time, the light of the stars needs time, deeds need time, even after they have been done, in order to be seen and heard. This deed is still further from men than the remotest stars—and yet they have done it.'

The story goes that the madman went into several churches on the same day, and sang his *requiem aeternam deo*. Led out and questioned, he replied just the one thing: 'What are the churches, if not the tombs and sepulchres of God?'[1]

Heidegger, in his essay on 'Nietzsche's words, "God is dead" ',[2] says that the words 'spell the destiny of two thousand years of western history'. He says that for Nietzsche 'God is the name for the realm of ideas and ideals'.[3] Whatever the justice of this remark, it is surely true that in Nietzsche's story we are confronted with experiential atheism as a realization of nothingness. This is nihilism in the same sense as Jean Paul's vision is nihilism.[4]

The distinction which we have drawn between what we

---

[1]*Fröhliche Wissenschaft*, no. 125.   [2]*Holzwege*, pp. 193–247.
[3]*op. cit.*, p. 199.
[4]Cf. Bultmann, 'Der Gottesgedanke und der moderne Mensch', *Zeitschrift für Kirche und Theologie*, December 1963, p. 337.

may call a procedural and an experiential atheism provides
the necessary clarity for assessing the present cult of what
has been called 'Death of God theology'. This is to be found
at its liveliest in a few American theologians, in particular
Thomas Altizer and William Hamilton. (The special
position of Paul van Buren, also an American theologian,
will be discussed later.) In spite of the vigour and sincerity
of their views, it is important to note that they are not
speaking of the simple and undialectical death of God. It
is only in one sense that God has withdrawn from the world.
Thus Hamilton writes:

In one sense God seems to have withdrawn from the
world and its sufferings, and this leads us to accuse
him of either irrelevance or cruelty. But in another
sense he is experienced as a pressure and a wounding
from which we would love to be free. For many of us
who call ourselves Christians, therefore, believing in the
'death of God' means that he is there when we do not
want him, and he is not there when we do want him.[1]

And in a recent essay, 'Thursday's Child: the Theologian
Today and Tomorrow', speaking of the estrangement of the
theologian from the church, he writes:

It used to be otherwise. Before, the theologian would
distinguish between God, Christendom, Christianity,
and church, so that a different balance of 'yes' and 'no'
could be uttered to each. Now he finds himself equally
alienated from each of the realities represented by the
four terms, and he says his 'no' to each. . .[2]

It is not through any desire to weaken the strength of
this 'no', but rather in order to give it its real place, that
I suggest that Hamilton (and even Altizer, with his more

[1] *New Essence of Christianity*, London, p. 69.
[2] *Theology Today*, January 1964, pp. 487–95.

extravagant statements[1]) are thinking essentially of the death of an *idea* of God, rather than speaking of the direct experience of the death of God. The passion of Nietzsche's nihilism has certainly affected all of us, and yet we must maintain the distinction we have made.

Furthermore, we must do this even though we also recognize that the whole issue is rendered infinitely complex by the historical reality of Christ's death. Certainly the man of faith cannot evade the source and the content of his faith, which is branded by that death. Whatever God is, whoever he is, for faith he is not other than Christ, who died. But it is in and through this death that we have *life*: he is, in and through death, the resurrection and the life. Thus the experience given to us in faith is an exceedingly complicated one: it is not direct, yet to faith it is radically true that in Christ death is absolute: absolute, yet also the way of life. So even if we may sympathize profoundly with the radical expression which these theologians give to their insight, it is questionable whether their dialectic of life in death is clearly enough stated.

Part of the unclarity at this point is undoubtedly due to the general unclarity which is to be found in the modern secularist position. For if we ask where this modern secular man is to be found, we must say plainly that he is every man. Of course he is various, in spite of the increasing collectivization of man, and the conformism which is its expression. So modern secular man can be empirically described in terms of many varying emphases. I myself

---

[1]In *Mircea Eliade and the Dialectic of the Sacred*, Philadelphia, 1963, e.g. p. 13: 'The first requirement . . . is a forthright confession of the death of the God of Christendom . . . Furthermore, we must recognise that the death of God is a historical event: God has died in *our* time, in *our* history, in *our* existence.'

have attempted elsewhere[1] to distinguish four principal 'images' of man which modern man may recognize in himself. Modern secular man is not a man apart, to whom the believer—or the moralist, or the educator, or any other established type—may speak as to one who is different from himself; but modern secular man is in each of us, so far as we live at all in our own time. The man who acknowledges for himself the radical significance of faith is not exempt from the conditions of his time. Chiefly this means that he is not exempt from the ambiguity of secularism. If he imagines that he is so exempt, or if he acts as if he were, or if he is indeed cut off from his time, entrenched in his dogmatic assurance, then he is not in the position of faith, but rather in the grip of that world of ideas which as Hegel saw was no longer effectively alive. The life of faith is one in which the other possibilities, and especially the secular possibility, play a real part. So we have not to envisage the situation of the man of faith as the one which has all the answers, which it has simply to convey to 'unbelief'. For the message of faith is not a possession of the believer. Rather, it is a claim upon him which he seeks to face responsibly in his own situation—and that situation includes the secularism of our whole age.

This has immense implications both for the form of religion and for the style of faith, as well as for the way in which the so-called 'communication' of the gospel is to be understood. It is not our purpose to pursue these implications into the practical sphere: it is enough to note that in the Protestant churches, where the dependence upon a few fixed dogmatic assumptions and certain social conventions has for so long dominated the style of faith, there

[1]In my essay, 'Post-Renaissance Man', in *Conflicting Images of Man*, ed. W. Nicholls, New York, 1965, where I distinguished the images of Adam, of religious man, of secular man, and of Christ as the New Man.

are at last signs of stirring. The work and writings of men like Gibson Winter in the United States and Bishop Wickham in England are heartening examples.[1] The Roman Catholic Church, which in its metaphysical assumptions has for long been so rigid, and yet so flexible and varied in its styles, is now in the midst of a movement which its friends outside will watch with the most attentive sympathy and hope.

In the absence, then, of any heteronomous metaphysic which is able to contain the message and the style of faith, and in the absence of any wish on the part of a radical theology to establish such a metaphysic, we may summarize what we have so far said about the relation of faith to the modern secular world by emphasizing that faith must move forward, without foresight, into a future which it welcomes as being without plan, without a fixed fate, out of a position where it freely recognizes its destiny in the present hour. And that destiny cannot circumvent the secularist world in which we are now all involved.

We have already noted that modern secularism is unwilling to recognize its origins as having anything more than a genetic interest. It wishes to have direct and unmediated enjoyment of its primary insight that man 'now runs his own life' (to use Gabriel Marcel's phrase for describing modern man's autonomy). Man can do anything that he wishes to do—and it is this autonomy which secularism claims to fulfil by denying the intrinsic relation to the structure of faith as we have analysed it in its biblical sources.

Now if our insistence upon this relation of secularism to faith were in fact to carry with it, what secularist man fears,

---

[1]See, e.g., Winter's *The Suburban Captivity of the Churches*, New York, and *The New Creation as Metropolis*, and Wickham's *Church and People in an Industrial City*, London, 1957.

a re-pristination of the old metaphysical heteronomy, then we should simply have to agree that this cannot be the way forward. That this however is not so, but that on the contrary faith is the very means of liberation, and of continued human freedom, is the whole burden of our reflections.

We shall have occasion to look again at the meaning of faith in its contrast with religion. Meantime, in terms of secularism itself, we may distinguish its inherent ambiguity at two points. First, there is a *malaise* in secularism which cannot be easily discounted. Certainly, this is an empirical observation, and as such is open to a variety of emphases and interpretations. But it cannot be disputed that there is a valid historical issue here. There is no denying the cogency of such a typical analysis as that of Max Scheler, when he writes:

In no other period of human knowledge has man ever become more problematic to himself than in our own day. We have a scientific, a philosophical and a theological anthropology that know nothing of each other. Therefore we no longer possess any clear and consistent idea of man. The ever-growing multiplicity of the particular sciences that are engaged in the study of man has much more confused and obscured than elucidated our concept of man.[1]

As illustrations of this lack of unity regarding the real nature of man we may think of man's breath-taking plans to reach the moon and the planets, and beyond, and of his simultaneous fear that he will not have the time to do so. We may recognize man's exhilarating freedom to shape his own society, and his simultaneous bondage to all kinds of ideologies. We may see him in his splendour as the mature and deliberate manipulator of nature and history, and at

[1] *Die Stellung des Menschen im Kosmos*, p. 13. Cf. Ernst Cassirer, *Essay on Man*, p. 22.

the same time we may see him in his misery, as a mere faceless number in the machinery of productivity, or as a bundle of *Angst*, without hope.

When we speak of this *malaise* in modern secularism as indicating its ambiguity, we do not mean to imply that secularism as such, authentic secularism, is incapable of coping with the spiritual confusion, the moral failure, and the unclarity concerning man's real nature which are characteristic of our society. For we should entirely agree with the secularist reply to the problems of our time. This reply takes, in general, two forms. First, it is maintained that even in our fearful modern predicaments there can be no going back: man must face his problems in the freedom and strength which are available to him as man. And secondly, it is maintained that we are only at the beginning of an unprecedented new life. In this expectation we cannot be surprised if we meet with confusion, and crises, mistakes and even far-reaching failures. No sudden and complete success can be expected in such a complex and revolutionary situation.

The ambiguity lies in the definition of the strength that is available to man. Again, we do not imply that faith wishes to intrude as the solver of problems or as the refuge in time of need. Of course it is true that many men will fall back on a childhood's prayer when they are faced with a grave personal or social problem. And it is not difficult to imagine a whole society running to the churches when life has got quite out of control. But to wait for or even more to encourage such a movement is the expression not of faith, but of despair, not of the free responsibility of secular man, but of superstition. Dr Raven's talk of 'baptizing' the new learning and the new society, to which we referred earlier,[1] so far as it implies such a 'spiritualizing' of the styles and

[1] See p. 148 above.

structures of modern secular society, must be discarded as a kind of face-saving operation on the part of the 'Christian forces'.

If, then, from the position of faith we wish neither to turn our backs on the secular attitude, nor to hope for a deepening of the crisis in order that a new (or one of the old) 'spiritual' attitudes may take over the control of man's life, what distinguishes the life of faith from that of the modern secularist?

The answer to this question is again complex, so that the rest of what we have to say in this book is really concerned with it. But we may make a start by noting the second and deeper ambiguity in modern secularism. This ambiguity lies in the contradiction between its claims and its covert means of substantiating these claims. It claims freedom for man, but provides him with bondage. It claims that responsibility is man's own, but it involves him ever more deeply in impersonal structures. It claims that a happy future lies ahead, but its means are nihilistic: they manipulate man for this glorious consummation, so that man himself is faced with *nihil*.

It is only in and through a radical secularism that we may both shape and be shaped by our true human destiny. Modern secularism is not secular enough. Radical secularism I shall distinguish from the unradical kind by calling it 'secularity'.

Modern secularism is not a clear structure at all. Rather it is a congeries of competing ideologies, or on the other hand it may be described as a creeping nihilism which takes various ideological or utopian forms. The nihilism becomes apparent when we see the basic form in which the ideologies are cast. These ideologies, whether the marxist, or the nationalist, or the racist, or the religious, or even the world-historical and universalist, are all alike in their inability

172

to contain the historical reality of man. They wish to contain man, but in doing so they deny the basic secular presupposition that man is solely and absolutely responsible for his own history. For they propose a scheme of development for man which is dependent not on man's own nature but on a view of the world. Their views of the world may be various, but basically they are at one in their proposal to substitute for man in his historical freedom a view of the world. They have the future under control—so they believe—for they have already anticipated it in their ideas. In this way they push man out of the centre of the picture: the human person, the willing, responsible, free human person, acting without foresight, open to the future which he can neither anticipate nor control, is displaced by a 'view' of man. Man as truly human disappears. His autonomy is essentially contradicted, not furthered, by these ideologies. His historical existence has been replaced by some form of collectivism. All these ideologies share the fearful assumption that man, individual man, the existing human person, is there to be managed and manipulated. The classic description of this for our time is to be found in George Orwell's *1984*.

So far as individual life is concerned, this replacement of historical man by any one of the proffered ideologies does not in the end produce any different result from that of direct nihilism: except that the defiant nihilism of Nietzsche, or the open-eyed nihilism of a man like Bertrand Russell, is more admirable and honest than the creeping nihilism of unhistorical and optimistic ideologies. Moreover, the ideologies always tend to relapse into some kind of religion, producing the horrid monster of an *ersatz* religion, re-divinizing some part of itself or its history, and providing even a bastard mythology and a bastard religiosity for its adherents.

What then has faith to say to this situation? Does it too not share the secularist dilemma? And is faith not pre-eminently tied up with religious forms, with mythologies and religiosity and the substitution of authentic secularity by an unrealistic optimism which is just another form of what I have called nihilist ideologies? In order to reach the point where we may try to understand the force of a truly secular faith, we must first clear the decks by looking at the relation between faith and religion.

5. *Faith not religion*

When Dietrich Bonhoeffer made his now famous remarks, in letters to his friend Eberhard Bethge, about the time of religion being over, and about how men simply cannot be religious any more, he was clearly not giving notice of an end to Christianity. On the contrary, the fragmentary suggestions which he made on the basis of the coming time in which there would be no religion at all are all concerned with the reality of Christianity.

Thus, in the first letter in which he broached these matters, after a whole year in prison, he writes:

I am constantly moved by the question what Christianity really is, or who Christ really is, for us today. The time in which everything could be said to men by means of words, whether theological or pious, is over. So too is the time of inwardness and conscience, which means the time of religion in general. We are moving towards a completely religionless time. Men as they now are simply cannot be religious any more . . . Our entire 1900-year-old Christian preaching and theology are based upon the religious *a priori* of men[1]

—and that *a priori*, he goes on to say, no longer exists as a viable historical possibility.

[1]30th April, 1944 (my translation). See *Widerstand und Ergebung*, Munich, 1951, p. 178; cf. *Letters and Papers from Prison*, Fontana ed., London, 1959.

Now he has a great deal more to say of what he means by religion, but it is important to see that from the outset of his reflections in the last letters what he is chiefly concerned about is not just a self-contained view of the world (namely, as without religion), but what Christianity and Christ really mean today. And in the earliest mention of the new 'religionless world'[1] he includes the question of how to speak of God in secular fashion. He is not merely raising a question of refurbished language to meet a new phase in the ongoing history of Christianity. But he is asking a radical question concerning God's being: how is it possible to speak of God at all in a world in which not only the old presuppositions, metaphysical, individualistic, and religious, are left out, but in which God himself is left out?

Bonhoeffer is not just rejecting a specific idea of God. Certainly, he gives short shrift to the *deus ex machina*, the god of the stop-gaps, both in intellectual argumentation and in moral crises—the god 'at the limits of human existence'. But his basic question goes further. It is the question how we may speak of God as transcendent, in a world which no longer admits the relevance of the old categories and the old sense of the transcendent. In other words, Bonhoeffer believes that he is facing a real crisis in the life of faith, which has never appeared before in all the 1900 years of Christian history.

Bonhoeffer goes on to define what he means by religion in a bewildering variety of ways. Religion means calling in God when human resources, intellectual or moral, are at an end, to solve otherwise insoluble problems. It means a metaphysical view of transcendence, what he also calls (in the *Ethics*) 'thinking in two spheres', the sphere of nature and the sphere of super-nature. It means individualistic

[1] 30th April, 1944.

piety, what he also calls 'methodism'. It means thinking of religion as a special compartment of one's life, or 'being religious in a particular way, by means of some method or other, making something of oneself (a sinner, a penitent or a saint).'[1] It is not simply identical with the law in the biblical sense. Certainly, the influence of Karl Barth is important, especially in his denunciation of religion as the enemy of Christianity in the sense of being the culmination of the law, regarded as the built-in human capacity to establish a relationship with God. But, if I may attempt to summarize Bonhoeffer's view, I should do it along the lines suggested by Dr Ebeling, that religion for Bonhoeffer means an attitude which regards man's life as being somehow completed by the addition of God. And this addition is variously regarded as an individual experience, an experience at the boundaries of human need, or the boundaries of human thought, or in some other way as an extension of the world or of the self.[2]

Now if we are to regard all this from a simply empirical standpoint we should, I think, have to modify Bonhoeffer's view considerably. *Homo religiosus* is still with us, and in us, in many different ways. Even beyond the empirical evidences of religiosity within the forms of Christianity there is still the important sense, to which I have already referred,[3] in which man is by no means free of religion today: in the sense, that is, in which he wishes to extend himself, that is, his idea of himself, into some absolute which is really just an extension of his world. This is the way in which modern ideologies express and extend their hold upon men.

[1] 18th July 1944.
[2] cf. Gerhard Ebeling, *Wort und Glaube*, pp. 145*f.* cf. English translation, *Word and Faith*, pp. 148*ff.*
[3] cf. p. 173 above.

But, as I say, Bonhoeffer is primarily concerned with the positive meaning of Christ and Christianity today. He recognizes man's movement towards religionlessness in more subtle terms than those of a passing or a recrudescent religiosity. For along with the idea of 'a time of no religion at all' we are presented with a conception of man's autonomy which is both an empirico-historical judgment, and something more. The something more I should define as a shift in the view of transcendence. The autonomy of man is at first sight a simple historical judgment:

The movement beginning about the 13th century . . . towards the autonomy of man (under which head I place the discovery of the laws by which the world lives and manages in science, social and political affairs, art, ethics, and religion) has in our time reached a certain completion. Man has learned to cope with all questions of importance without recourse to God as a working hypothesis . . . As in the scientific field, so in human affairs generally 'God' is being more and more driven out of life, losing more and more ground.[1]

This is the adulthood or coming of age of the world. But the significance of this change for Bonhoeffer is not in an undialectical maturity of man, but once again in the question of God.

There are several indications in the letters that even in a straightforward empirical sense Bonhoeffer by no means regards this autonomy as simply analogous to an individual's maturity. In the following little-regarded passage we see how a theological judgment is clearly implied:

Once more I have started reading the *Losungen* [an annual volume of texts published by the Moravians] and meditated upon them (Numbers 11.23 and II Corinthians 1.23) ['And the Lord said to Moses, Is the

[1] 8th June 1944.

Lord's hand shortened? Now you shall see whether my word will come true for you or not. For all the promises of God find their Yes in him. That is why we utter the Amen through him, to the glory of God']. Surely everything depends on the 'in him'. All that we may rightly expect and pray for from God is to be found in Jesus Christ. All that a God as we think of him ought to do and could do—with this the God of Jesus Christ has nothing to do. We must again and again sink ourselves, at length and in quietness, in the life, sayings, deeds, suffering and death of Jesus, in order to know what God promises and fulfils . . . Again and again in these turbulent times we lose sight of why it is really worth living. We think that life only has meaning for us because this or that man is living. But the truth is that if the earth deserved to have the man Jesus Christ, if a man like Jesus lived, then and then only is there any meaning in life for us men . . .[1]

What is the implication of this intense christocentric faith for Bonhoeffer's view both of the maturity of the world and of a time of no religion? The implication is twofold. First, the autonomy of the world is given in Christian faith. And second, the world cannot understand itself unless it recognizes its relation to Christian faith.

First, the autonomy of the world is given in Christian faith. This means that while Bonhoeffer's empirico-historical assessment places the movement towards the world's coming of age somewhere towards the end of the middle ages (which I myself should be inclined to date more precisely with the songs of the troubadours, especially of Bernard de Ventadour, who flourished about the middle of the twelfth century), his understanding of faith enables him, indeed compels him, to place this movement in the very

[1] 21st August 1944.

179

heart of Christianity. That is to say, it is the life of Christ himself which liberates the world. Man, that is, the man of faith, 'may live in a "worldly" way, i.e. he is freed from false religious bonds and inhibitions'.[1] Or again, 'the only way to be honest is to recognize that we have to live in the world *etsi deus non daretur*.'[2]

Now this is not a straightforward autonomy of the world. It is therefore not to be understood as an objective truth, standing by itself, as it were, simply the truth of the self-contained and sovereign reality of the world. It is therefore a misreading of Bonhoeffer simply to write off the whole movement of Christian faith in the world as being merely the occasion for establishing the world in its maturity. Faith is not the scaffolding by which we have been able to rise to this height, which may then be knocked away, leaving the structure of the world in solitary power over itself. A great deal of misunderstanding clusters round this side of Bonhoeffer's ideas. And it is true that Bonhoeffer himself never had the time to make the clear connexions of thought between the various fragmentary utterances of the letters.

But the distinctions are implicit, all the same, in what he does say. He would surely have agreed with van Leeuwen's words, that 'secularization may be broadly described as the creative and liberating activity of the Word of God'.[3] And with his clear and steady love for the Old Testament we may add that he would surely also have agreed that there too we may see the secularizing power of faith at work. The bible is not a religious book, or books. The struggle of Israel's faith is a constant struggle with religion. The bible does not tire of telling how even man's most

---

[1] 18th July 1944.   [2] 16th July 1944.
[3] A. T. van Leeuwen, *Christianity in World History*, London, 1964, p. 332.

splendid achievements cannot reach God, or even touch him. And from a spectator's point of view the most obvious thing about the story of Israel's manipulation of powers in order to reach God is the monotony of their failure. It is not in their religious aspirations that Israel finds God. But rather, even in their failure they discover that there is a 'nevertheless'. Nevertheless their God is with them and for them. Nevertheless the people lived in and with the faith that God was active in their history. They did not need to search for God, they did not need to prove his existence, for he was already there, and had found them. Not that this meant they had a place of safety, such as in their religious aspirations they hoped to find. But they were simply seized by a conviction which launched them on an unpredictable course.

But secondly, for Bonhoeffer the autonomous world cannot understand itself unless it recognizes its relation to this faith. As he clearly says, 'the world's coming of age is no longer an occasion for polemics and apologetics',[1] and the 'driving of God out of life'[2] is wrongly understood as 'a great defection from God'. But as he also says, this 'maturity of the world is really better understood than it understands itself, namely, from the standpoint of the Gospel, of Christ'.[3] And in the next letter (not, alas! the promised 'instalments of theology' which were to be written the following day, but which have not survived), dated 21st June 1944, there is a brief word of appreciation for a book by W. F. Otto of Königsberg, in which Bonhoeffer quotes Otto's closing words, 'this world of faith, which sprang from the wealth and depth of human existence, rather than from its cares and longings'. Here too it is not too great a leap from this reference to the view of faith which I have been suggesting, a faith, namely, which arises in the midst of the historical

[1] 8th June 1944.   [2]*ibid.*   [3]*ibid.*

creative activity of man, not on the borders of human existence but in the midst of life.

The crux of the matter for Bonhoeffer lies in the way in which we recognize our maturity. We do not simply live in the world *etsi deus non daretur*, as though God were not given. But we live in this way—'before God'. And Bonhoeffer goes on, with perhaps the most significant of all his remarks in this matter:

God himself compels us to recognize this. So our coming of age leads us to a true recognition of our situation before God. God gives us to know that we must live as men who manage our lives without God. The God who is with us is the God who forsakes us. [And here he refers us to Mark 15.34, Christ's words on the cross, 'My God, my God, why hast thou forsaken me?' Then he goes on:] The God who lets us live in the world without the working hypothesis of God is the God before whom we are ever standing. Before God and with God we live without God. God lets himself be driven out of the world on to the cross. God is powerless and weak in the world, and that is precisely the way, the only way, in which he is with us and helps us. Matthew 8.17 [the words of Isaiah, 'Himself took our infirmities, and bare our sicknesses'] makes it quite clear that Christ does not help in virtue of his omnipotence, but by his weakness and suffering.[1]

With these words, as it seems to me, Bonhoeffer points to the source of the movement towards the liberation of the world, and to the present actuality of that source in the hidden presence of God. With these words must be directly linked what he also has to say about the arcane or hidden discipline of faith.

One important question still has to be faced. It may well

[1] 16th July 1944.

be asked by the modern secularist whether after all I have not merely shown that Bonhoeffer, for all his forward-looking faith (and, incidentally, the decisions he took in the ordinary course of his life as a consequence of that faith, which joined him with ordinary secular men in the conspiracy against Hitler, as well as with men like Moltke) is not just re-introducing here a new apologetic, and a variation on the old religious theme. Is he after all saying anything substantially different from all the other theologians who wish to claim everything for a specific idea of God? So, is his time of no religion at all not just a restoration, a highly sophisticated and veiled restoration, of all the old traditional material of Christianity?

Unfortunately Bonhoeffer never reached the point in his reflections where he was able to present a complete re-interpretation of biblical concepts. He planned to do it, and one of the last things he wrote was a few pages which he entitled 'Sketch of a Work'. I select the outstanding points from that sketch:

Man is once more cast upon himself. He has managed to deal with everything, only not with himself . . . What is God? Not in the first place a general belief in God, in his omnipotence, etc. This is not a genuine experience of God, but a piece of extended world. Meeting with Jesus Christ. The experience that a transformation of all human life is given in the fact that 'Jesus is there only for others.' Jesus 'being there for others' is the experience of transcendence . . . Faith is the participation in this being of Jesus . . . Our relation to God is not a 'religious' relation to some supreme, almighty, best of all beings—this is not genuine transcendence—but our relation to God is a new life in 'being there for others', in participation in the being of Jesus. Transcendence is not infinite and unattainable tasks, but it is the accessible neighbour, who is given to us again and again. God in human form . . . 'the man for others', and hence the Crucified. The man who lives from transcendence.[1]

Now it seems to me clear beyond dispute that in such a passage we are being given a glimpse of something radically different from the old forms of religion. Of course it is inchoate, and elusive, and enigmatic. And it leaves many questions about Bonhoeffer's ultimate view still unsettled. But I have chosen to spend so long on an analysis of what is available of Bonhoeffer's views because it seems to me that we are presented here with a highly charged, extremely dialectic, and radical Christianity, which faces the mystery of human existence with a real historical hope. The analysis of man is made with the utmost freedom, and it never at any point relapses into an ideology which would remove man from the centre of the picture. And the point at which he might be charged with attempting a restoration of old formulas is precisely the point at which he is advancing beyond both unradical modern secularism and religious formulations of faith: I mean in his view of transcendence. This is the point where the real movement away from religion (and unradical secularism) into a time of no religion takes its start.

In what I have already said about transcendence in terms of our understanding of God's action[2] I have gone beyond Bonhoeffer's hints. Here I need only repeat that transcendence is to be recognized as an event which happens to us, as Bonhoeffer says, 'in the accessible neighbour, who is given to us again and again.'

This is the way in which we may begin to speak of God

[1]My translation, *Widerstand und Ergebung*, p. 259, cf. *Letters and Papers from Prison*, Fontana ed. p. 164*f*.

[2]See above, pp. 121*ff*.

in the secular language of faith. This is more than a transposition of theology into the practical life, excluding any talk about God. But the possibility of God-language is a lively present issue for itself in modern theology, to which we must now turn.

6. *God-language*

As we have just seen, Bonhoeffer's concern in his last letters could be described as the possibility of God-language. And, as I understand him, this possibility is still a real one. His theology cannot be circumscribed as 'the man for others', but if we extract this phrase from his last writings, we must not forget to add the next phrase, 'the man who lives from transcendence'.

One more quotation from Bonhoeffer's letters will help us not to interpret the possibility of God-language too narrowly. On 5th May 1944, he writes:

It is not with the next world that we are concerned, but with this world as created and preserved and made subject to laws and atoned for and made new. What is above the world is intended, in the Gospel, to exist *for* the world . . . in the bible sense of the creation, incarnation, crucifixion and resurrection of Jesus Christ.

Bonhoeffer, it will be noted, is here still able to talk about 'what is above the world'. I should myself not be able to speak in terms of this spatial metaphor. But it is more than a matter of metaphor. I have already spoken of transcendence as an event which happens to us, and in particular of the transcendence of God as the faith in his absolute otherness given to us in his historical being for us in Christ.

Transcendence on this view is a thoroughly historical experience.

The trend of theological fashion at present, however, is less dialectical than this. On first view it is most attractive and straightforward. Paul van Buren's work, *The Secular Meaning of the Gospel*, London, 1963, is an impressive contribution to the whole discussion. But though the kernel of his argument bears a family resemblance to the ideas of Bonhoeffer, in the end we must judge that it is an instructive, because unintentional, warning against too undialectical an understanding of the kerygma.

Van Buren agrees, he says, with Bultmann, that 'the whole tenor of thought of our world today makes the biblical and classical formulations of this Gospel unintelligible.'[1] After a brilliant analysis of patristic christological thought he has this revealing remark: 'When modern theologians define the humanity of Jesus as his being-for-others, his involvement with and compassion for his fellow men, they speak as men who are interested in history and find it a more helpful paradigm than nature for understanding man'[2]. Further, 'if they [the patristic theologians] had been more consistent in saying that God is unknown apart from his self-revelation and that we must begin with Jesus Christ in order to know anything about God at all, they might have been able to begin with the cross as the event of the self-revelation of a God who is quite able to take suffering to himself and whose glory is so great that he can also humble himself.'[3]

It soon becomes clear, however, that the christo-centrism of such remarks is really better described as Jesu-centrism. For van Buren falls back on what I can only call the naive empiricism of some analytic philosophers, with whose help he is able to assert that 'the non-objective use of the word

[1] *op. cit.*, p. 6. [2] *op. cit.*, p. 41. [3] *op. cit.*, p. 42.

"God" allows of no verification and is therefore meaning-less'.[1] And this impossibility of using the word 'God' 'non-objectively' implies for van Buren that any kind of analogical speaking about God is *ipso facto* a cognitive approach, which 'requires speaking about that which it admits is ineffable'.[2] He is therefore prepared to abandon any straightforward use of the word 'God'.[3] There is in fact no room left for talking about God at all. God-language is meaningless.

Then what is left? Van Buren still finds a meaning in the language of faith. It is the meaning implied by what R. M. Haire has called a '*blik*' conception of faith. That is, 'statements of faith are to be interpreted, by means of the modified verification principle, as statements which express, describe, or commend a particular way of seeing the world, other men, and oneself, and the way of life appropriate to such a perspective.'[4]

This particular way of seeing the world is derived from the Christian norm, that is, from the 'series of events to which the New Testament documents testify, centering in the life, death and resurrection of Jesus of Nazareth'.[5]

But when we ask what then this norm enables us to see, we hear that 'if love for the neighbour is the test of love for God, then by the verification principle it is the meaning of the "love for God".'[6] In this way van Buren clearly wishes to reduce Christianity to what he calls its 'historical and ethical dimensions', as indeed he himself admits.[7]

Now in the analysis of these historical and ethical dimensions of Christianity van Buren has striking and illuminating insights. His description of Jesus as the only truly free man, both free from anxiety and free for his neighbour, is

[1]*op. cit.*, p. 83.   [2]*op. cit.*, p. 98.   [3]*op. cit.*, p. 100.
[4]*op. cit.*, p. 156.   [5]*op. cit.*, p. 156.   [6]*op. cit.*, p. 183.
[7]*op. cit.*, pp. 197*ff.*

by no means without attractive power. And his description of what happened to the disciples at Easter as being that 'they came to share in this freedom to be for others'[1] is also not without a certain edifying power.

But to sum up the gospel as 'the story of the free man who had set them free'[2] really lets the cat out of the bag. If van Buren were as respectful towards the whole hermeneutical debate concerning the history of Jesus, the nature of the kerygma, and the form-critical issues, as he is towards the analytic philosophers, he could never be content with this attenuated and undialectical summary. Throughout his account of the so-called 'historical and ethical dimensions' he seems to be entirely unconscious of the dialectic, which I have analysed earlier, of our relation to past events in their paradoxical presence. Of the eschatological insights of recent theology he has only this to say: 'More difficult, however, is the problem of an appeal to eschatological verification . . . no one knows the empirical attitudes which would be either possible in or appropriate to the *eschaton*'[3] —the *eschaton*, apparently, as mythologically conceived. Again and again we come up against the blank wall of the appeal to the verification principle. Thus the Easter assertion, 'Jesus is risen', can only be verified 'by the conduct of the man who uses it'.[4] The possibility that faith is a part of the historical reality of the kerygma is not seriously raised.

Is this the necessary outcome of dropping the categories of substance for the understanding of transcendence? Even if we agree with van Buren that 'the language of faith, by referring to a transcendent element, indicates that something has happened to the believer, rather than that he has done something',[5] can this something be reduced to what he calls the 'contagion' of Jesus' freedom? What view of history lies behind this summary expression, 'contagion'? It

[1] p. 132.   [2] p. 134.   [3] p. 98.   [4] p. 132.   [5] p. 141.

seems that van Buren, in his anxiety to keep within the confines prescribed by a would-be 'empirical' attitude, has been forced back into a refined pietism. The paradoxical claim of the kerygma that in Christ God is present to faith has been removed of any possible offence: in effect, we are here offered a piece of liberal cake, somewhat stale, indeed, but freshened up by the sauce of empirical verification. The resemblances to the 'influence' theory of Martin Kähler, or even to the Herrmann theory of the 'inward' personality of Jesus as carrying its own authentication, are strong enough to suggest that van Buren has simply not faced the reality of the paradox or of the demand for faith.

When this is said, however, it is still necessary to ask what can be said of God that is not somehow being said of Jesus.

Now Bonhoeffer, as we have seen, comes very near to saying what van Buren openly does say, namely, that John 14.9–10 ('He who has seen me has seen the Father') is to be interpreted as 'whatever men were looking for in looking for "God" is to be found by finding Jesus of Nazareth.'[1] But Bonhoeffer does not fall into this psychologizing trap. For while he talks of Jesus as 'the man for others' (which van Buren has taken back one step by talking of Jesus as 'the free man'), he does not exhaust his definition of transcendence in this summary of the kerygma. 'This concern of Jesus for others is the experience of transcendence' —certainly: but, Bonhoeffer goes on, 'our relation to God is not a religious relation . . . but a new life in the "being there for others", through participation in the Being of Jesus.'[2] Everything that Bonhoeffer says brings us clearly before the message concerning Jesus; but equally, it brings us before the possibility of a relation to God. Everything is

[1] p. 147.
[2] *Widerstand und Ergebung*, p. 259; cf. *Letters and Papers from Prison*, p. 165.

concentrated in the life of Jesus; but everything is simultaneously the reality of God.

Now Bonhoeffer, as we have seen, does not do more than state the simultaneities. The problem of expression remains. And with a great deal of what van Buren has to say about reticence and silence we are in hearty agreement. Yet, with all the reserve that is required of us at this point, it still seems to me to be essential, in face of the reality of history, that we should attempt the impossible, and somehow speak both of God and of man, both of the being of the transcendent God and of the historical existence of Jesus Christ.

This impossible possibility can only be attempted in the very terms of the message concerning Jesus. We do not propose to offer any separate christology as a substitute for the magnificent failures of the traditional formulations. What we offer is the paradox of the simultaneity of God's being in action with his being for us in Christ. Here we must agree whole-heartedly with van Buren about the necessity for silence about God 'in himself', and thus for a full negative theology. But neither of these necessities leads us into the assertion of absence of meaning in the 'transcendent God'.

As we have seen, no view of transcendence which leaves God cut off from his world is able to cope with the Christian kerygma. It is in his historicity that God is met in the call to faith. This 'meeting' is not the same as 'knowing' in the sense of the result of a piece of discursive reasoning. Far less can it be thought of as the affirmation of an isolated self, knowing itself, and then deducing the existence of another. But so far as it may be called knowing it is the acknowledgment in faith of a historical reality. It is a historical decision, it is the way in which we acknowledge the presence of a claim upon our life rising up out of the past. This past is

the past of Jesus, as presented to us in the message concerning
him. But it is not simply and immediately a 'knowing' of
Jesus (whether as 'free', or 'for others', or as carrying unique
'authority' or 'Messianic consciousness', etc.). Along this
line we sooner or later end in the quicksands of subjectivism
or relativism, or both. It is not an immediate or direct
knowing at all. But it is a decision concerning our life in
its relation to the past, and for its future. And this decision
carries within it the ineluctable affirmation of the reality of
God. But this affirmation is never separated from the way
in which the decision is made—namely, in face of the
message concerning Jesus. It is thus an affirmation simultaneously of the absolute historicity of God, and of the reality
of God's being for us as the way in which God is. We cannot
at this point as it were cast off into the sea of God's being:
there is no being of God for us other than his being-for-us
in Christ. But this is his reality. He is constantly himself,
and is never other than he is in Christ. But this constant
remaining himself is known to us in the historical realizing
of himself which is present to us in the kerygma—that is, is
present again and again to us in the presentation of the
kerygma.

So God is always himself, but the self which he always is
is a self which is constantly present in history. We may
perhaps speak here of permanence in change, permanence
through change. But this terminology smacks of an idealist
conceptuality which envisages God's reality as somehow
located in a realm of ideal values, and his historical appearances, therefore, as bearing about them just a whiff of
docetism. The contrary must be affirmed: the reality of
God is his historical reality, any talk of God as abstracted
from history casts a slur, however slight, upon his reality.
His reality, what has sometimes been called his 'Is-ness', can
never be expressed by us, as it can never be encountered

and thus known by us, other than in terms of his historical being for us.

Thus we may certainly, and gladly, affirm the necessity for a christo-led understanding of God. But this understanding cannot rest in Jesus as a figure of the past (however subtle the exegesis), and not even in the kerygma when the kerygma is regarded as a self-contained entity which can be transposed without remainder into a set of teachings about Christ. Nor can it be transposed into a realm of ideals, of permanence above and beyond the historical actualities—not even into eternity, for all that we know of eternity is what is present to us now in the acceptance of faith. 'God not in the conceptual forms of the absolute, the metaphysical, the infinite, etc. . . . but "the man for others", and hence the Crucified One.'[1] But, let it be repeated, it is *God* who is 'the man for others'.

[1]Bonhoeffer, *op. cit.*, p. 260; cf. Fontana ed., p. 165.

7. Secular Christianity

What has so far emerged in this section on secularism is a series of distinctions: outside and inside secularism, outside and inside Christianity: and especially the distinction between faith and religion (viewed as an addition or completion of man's existence by means of an idea of God as the answer to a moral need or an intellectual question); the distinction between the secularity of faith and the secularism which is based upon a philosophy or world-view which tries to anticipate the future in an ideology; and lastly, we may add, as implicit in the story of the West, the distinction between the reality of Christ and the Christendom which is the reaction to that reality. By Christendom here I mean simply the effects or deposits of Christian faith in historical structures, experiences, and ideas. I do not mean the once unbroken structure of mediaeval society, the memory of which now often serves merely to foster the illusion that a similar structure may be again attained by a kind of restoration of the past.

These distinctions, however, do not mean that there are separations in reality. Christian faith in its radical secularity, and with its basic reference to Christ as God's historical being-for-man, is not relieved by these necessary distinctions from its connexions with religion, with secularism, and with Christendom. In so far as all the structures, of religion, of secularism, and of Christendom as a whole, partake of historical freedom they are the inevitable partners of faith. For faith lives in and by history. It is not only, as we have seen, historical in its source, but it also takes form in historical structures. And just as there can be no 'pure' theology, and no absolute or permanent form of faith, separated from the untidy, ambiguous and distorting forms of man's historical existence, in all its vicissitudes, so faith is bound to be expressed, and thus communicated, in these same forms.

It is faith's care to exercise a constant critique of these forms, of the religious forms against which it must protest and which it must again and again overcome; of the secularist forms so that it exposes their unradical nature with its permanent threat of inhumanity; and of the styles and structures of Christendom, so that they may never arrogate to themselves any claim to inviolability, or infallibility, or sanctity. It must be faith's care to criticize and protest against all these forms, in order that the historical unrest of faith, its necessary openness to the future, may be safeguarded.

For the forms and structures of religion and secularism and Christendom are never able to express directly the historical freedom which is the heart of the existence of faith. For they partake of necessity, of fate, and of a constant temptation to misunderstand their own place and possibilities. They contain within themselves the movement leading to their self-destruction, and the destruction of all that is joined to them: the movement into a false and premature autonomy, away from freedom, from the possibility of truly personal life, from the world of Thou to the world of It, from the decision for the open future to the decision for a closed and self-contained existence.

This is the mystery of the wrong choice, which is the presence of evil in the world. So powerful is the attraction of this movement towards self-destruction that it is not beyond the bounds of possibility that it will carry mankind, with its brief and fragmentary experience of freedom, into total destruction. Historical freedom is a fragile shoot, planted with difficulty, amid uncertain and uncongenial conditions, and easily destroyed by neglect or opposition. It has indeed flourished only intermittently, and rarely, in the whole story of mankind.

What then are we to conclude concerning the form and style of faith, its content and its communication? How are we to understand the problem of the 'mission' of Christianity, or the widespread desire for 'Christian action', for the carrying of the gospel into the world? Is any clear outline discernible?

Now one particular answer, though much desired, often attempted, and usually considered the ideal answer, cannot be given. In the light of the distinctions we have drawn we cannot look for the expression of faith in unitary and un-dialectical form in the structures of history. No man and no society can reproduce faith in absolute purity and directness. Any claim on the part of a historical church to be that pure expression is a confused and confusing mis-understanding. The misunderstanding rests upon the basic error of supposing that faith may indeed have a fixed and visible form and structure with a specific and verifiable content. This is not possible just because faith is at no point able to anticipate the future. This is the tragic melancholy inherent in the reality of faith, that it has no fixed future which it may draw into its present forms. Faith does have a form peculiar to itself: but it is the form of hope, of expectation, of patient waiting upon the future which is given to it again and again by God. This is the style of faith, and it forbids us to demand or to expect any permanent and identifiable expression. Or we may put it the other way round, and say that faith is ready for all and every expression: faith is readiness: whatever comes in the course of the ongoing—or even of the no-longer-ongoing —structures of society is grist to faith's mill. For faith is a perpetually recurring possibility of action in a world which is entirely unpredictable, and which faith helps to keep unpredictable.

But of course, in terms of relative action and the necessary entry into the concrete situation a great deal could be said. And it is one of the encouraging signs of the life of our time that thought and reflective decisions are emerging here and there, both inside and outside the circle of the organized churches. It is not our intention to expound these practical matters here. But if my reflections as a whole are considered to be just, then clearly they must also be timely. I leave it to the reflective decisions of my readers to find their own place, and thus their own special relationship to faith's historicity, in the midst of the questions that await decision.

Nevertheless a little can be said here, by way of illustration. First, I accept gladly the analysis by Gibson Winter in the work to which I have already referred, *The New Creation as Metropolis*. There he speaks of the three forms of the church, first, as a cultic body, second, as a confessing assembly, and third, as a prophetic fellowship.[1] Perhaps the cultic body and the confessing assembly may even be put more closely together than Mr Winter does, as representing activities which both look to the past, and in the strength of the past, by cultic re-enactment or by the proclamation of the sacred narrative, seek to preserve a place for themselves in the present. Characteristic of these two groups is their interest to preserve their own strength,

[1]New York, 1963. See especially chapter iii, 'The Prophetic Fellowship'.

their visible, institutional power. The symbol of the cultic body is the priest looking to the altar, from which he receives and dispenses the elements of salvation. The symbol of the confessing assembly is the preacher raised above the people, facing them and proclaiming to them in God's name the message he has received. The symbol of the prophetic fellowship is a little anonymous group, looking together at their own particular problem. They are not necessarily without the support either of the cult or the confession. But essentially they are engaged in theological reflection in the context of a call for action. They may have the help of a theological specialist, but such specialists are rare. In any case, the prophetic fellowship has to face its own problems in the light of what it is learning of responsible action, in faith, in a given situation. It is essentially a lay fellowship, that is, literally, a company of the *people* of God. It may or may not have the traditional marks of the church which are the 'possession' of the cultic body and the confessing assembly—the dispensing of the sacraments and the proclamation of the Word of God. There is a moving description in Horst Symanowski's striking book, *The Christian Witness in an Industrial Society*, in which a group, in the midst of a struggle to reach their decision about a particular problem, find themselves driven to the need for the Lord's Supper: and so, round the bare discussion table, with elements drawn from the kitchen of the house, one of their number, one of the people, a layman, celebrates the sacrament.[1] At least, if a prophetic fellowship does have these 'marks' it has them without self-concern, and not as a possession for their spiritual nurture or individual edification. For the point of their being together is that they are looking not to themselves, but they are looking together at the call to action.

[1]Philadelphia, 1964; London, 1966. See pp. 84*f*.

These lay groups, appearing more or less spontaneously in many forms (e.g. Evangelical Academies in Europe, Frontier groups, and factory and business fellowships), bear the burden and the hope for faith today. They are not opposed to the church in its institutional forms. But they are responding to the situation, especially in what Mr Winter calls 'metropolis', the urban form of our society with its many distinct planes of work, in terms of that situation itself. They are to be found where people work. In the suburbs, to which on the whole the institutional and traditional forms of the church have withdrawn, there is certainly work for the church as well. But in the main this needs to be extended into various forms of pastoral counselling, especially for the women who dominate the styles of suburban life, opening windows for them to allow them to come out of their illusory world.

In this complex situation, which I have done no more than indicate, it would also follow that the forces of the official churches are in urgent need of re-deployment. As a corollary to this, the education for the ministry needs to be entirely re-modelled. The movement in many places away from the seminary and out into the universities is a healthy sign. It would be even healthier if the seminary did not merely carry its methods and load of instruction into the universities, as a separate faculty, but were a real part of the society of the university—which is, on the whole, best understood, in its problems as well as its possibilities, as a miniature of the world.

To return to the main course of our reflections, we have necessarily been speaking of the formal outline of the historicity of faith. The very nature of faith as the spontaneous engagement with history precludes more than the most tentative remarks about how this engagement is worked out in concrete situations. Each individual, each group, each fellowship, must find its own way in its own situation.

But the outline of faith appears as the very means of true secularity. Faith is not concerned to proselytize. It cannot proselytize, because it carries no equipment, and peddles no wares, which it may offer to the passer-by. Its only way is to carry in the body, that is, in the historical existence in the world which it both maintains and endures, the marks of Jesus. But these marks are not sacred stigmata of the kind the crowd longs to see and touch. They are the marks of absolute openness, which is absolutely engaged with the historical possibilities of the hour. So faith is never 'beyond tragedy', for the future to which it lies open, and to which it looks in hope, is not yet accomplished. The 'not yet' of St Paul's words ('Not as though I had already attained, either were already perfect: but I follow after, if that I may apprehend that for which also I am apprehended of Christ Jesus'[1]) is the refrain which runs through the whole song of faith. The End in Christ is here and now in our present history only in the form of faith's openness to the future.

So faith has no fixed expression. The desire for such an expression is the ever-present temptation to substitute sight for faith. The secularity of faith can therefore not aim at 'making' Christians—or Presbyterians or Roman Catholics or any specific brand of 'Christian'—and not even at making saints. Bonhoeffer has put the matter well, in a letter of 21st July 1944:

Later I experienced, and I am experiencing it to this day, that one learns to have faith only in complete this-worldliness of life. When one has entirely given up making something of oneself—whether a saint or a converted sinner or a churchman (a so-called priestly figure), a righteous or an unrighteous man, a sick man or a healthy man—and this is what I call this-worldli-

[1] Philippians, 3.11.

ness, namely, to live in the fulness of the tasks, questions, successes and failures, experiences and helplessness—then one throws oneself into God's arms, entirely, then one no longer takes one's own sufferings seriously, but the suffering of God in the world, then one watches with Christ in Gethsemane, and I think that is faith, *metanoia*, and so one becomes a man, a Christian (cf. Jeremiah 45).

Faith, in other words, is open, ever again open, through sorrow and repentance, to the possibility of true personal life. The secularity of faith means that it is through and through a worldly affair. But this worldliness of faith is kept from introversion and self-pity by the dialectic of creatureliness. Only in the acknowledgment of themselves as creatures can men be truly themselves. This is the profundity of the wisdom which Bonhoeffer found at that moment, the day after the last attempt on Hitler's life, the great conspiracy, had failed. It is worth quoting in full the chapter of Jeremiah to which he refers:

. . . Thus saith the Lord, the God of Israel, unto thee, O Baruch; Thou didst say, Woe is me now! For the Lord hath added grief to my sorrow; I fainted in my sighing, And I find no rest. Thus shalt thou say unto him, The Lord saith thus; Behold, that which I have built will I break down, And that which I have planted I will pluck up, Even this whole land. And seekest thou great things for thyself? Seek them not: For, behold, I will bring evil upon all flesh, saith the Lord. But thy life will I give unto thee for a prey in all places whither thou goest.

But, it may still be said, if faith is thus entirely open to the future, which is unpredictable, if it is without verifiable content or fixed and visible form, then several serious questions are still unanswered. What of our view of Providence?

What of the 'fruit' of the Spirit? And what of the relation of faith to the form of Christ in the world? And all these questions might be summed up in the anxious question, 'Is faith then entirely invisible?'

Now there is a profound sense in which the answer to this summary question can only be Yes. Faith is not discernible. It is not available as a specific objectified entity in the world. Faith is never an It in the world of It. At this point Bonhoeffer's seldom regarded insistence upon the discipline of the hidden or arcane life is of the utmost significance as a symbol of what is here true of faith. Faith is a flower that blossoms in secret, being tended in secret, and wanting no other air and light and nourishment than that which comes from the end of all things in the perfect will of God.

But if this flower is in heaven, its roots are nevertheless struck deep in the earth. And so we cannot rest in the thought of faith's eschatological reality as a simple comfort. For this eschatological reality is at the same time present, it is in the present hour as the anticipation of the end.

In what way, then, may we speak of the presence of faith, in what way are we to understand the fruit of the Spirit, or the form of Christ in the world? And are we not bound to say more of the manifestation of the Providence of God in history than we have so far been able to say?

With certain reservations we are able to concur with the following striking remarks by Karl Barth, which I give in full:

In faith in God's providence man will certainly look into *history* with very open, very attentive, very participating eyes. How could it be otherwise? ... It would not be faith which was not also in this regard *knowledge*—relative, provisional, modest, in need of correction, but real, thankful and courageous knowledge. He who believes in God's providence does not only know *in abstracto* and in general that God is over all and that everything is in God's hands. But he always gets to *see*, again and again, something of the work of these hands, he may also, again and again, perceive God's will and purposes in quite definite happenings, relations, connexions and changes in the history of creaturely being. He *notices* in it determinations and leadings, hints and signs, boundaries which are set and possibilities which are opened, threats and judgments, gracious preservations and help. He knows how to *distinguish* between great and small, truth and appearance, promises and perils. He also knows how to distinguish . . . action and suffering, struggle and peace. He *is aware* again and again that the hour has struck, and he acts accordingly.[1]

The reservations we must introduce here are that, even with all this knowing, seeing, distinguishing and so on, which Barth italicizes, we must not fall into the error of attempting a 'general' interpretation of history in the light of our faith in God's providence. We cannot objectify this faith in any form. The signs which are visible are always visible to faith alone. That is to say, they are not visible as objects in the world at all. They cannot be used to prove faith to be true, or to buttress it in time of need or despair. They are crutches which faith longs to keep, but which it must throw away if it is to be itself. Faith grows stronger only as it suffers, not as it triumphs in the substitution of sight for faith. For the only way of faith is that of hope and love. But neither the hope nor the love is a triumph, but the tentative makeshift form of a suffering faith.

What then of the fruit of the Spirit in the life of the man of faith, and in the life of the society of faith? Clearly, this fruit is not restricted to the casual catalogue which St Paul

[1] *Kirchliche Dogmatik*, III/3 pp. 25 *f.* cf. *Church Dogmatics* III/3, p. 23.

gives in Galatians 5.22*f.*: 'love, joy, peace, longsuffering, gentleness, goodness, faith (=fidelity), meekness and temperance.' These are given as the signs of the end: they are the illustration of the style of faith in the world. They are the result of the paradoxical union of the end in Christ with the ongoing life of faith in this world. They are therefore all marked by the way of God in the world. They are signs of the form which God's life takes. But they are not specific blueprints for Christian 'action' vis-à-vis the world. We cannot define any concerted action which could claim to be the manifest Christian course of action. For in the last resort Christian action is determined by the mode of suffering. And the mode of suffering has infinite possibilities of expression.

The reality of secular Christianity is therefore very different both from an undialectical assertion of the triumph of God in the world and an equally undialectical assertion of the maturity of the world. It cannot be expressed either in terms of the simple presence or the simple absence of God. But secular Christianity means the dialectical expression of the presence of the Spirit, which is the way of Christ in the world, in forms which can be neither objectively distinguished nor enumerated. The form of Christ in the world is certainly a historical reality: it is *the* historical reality. It is the prolepsis of the End. But this historical reality cannot be pinned down. The theology of faith is a theology of the cross, and thus a *theologia viatorum*. It is a theology of a pilgrim journey which makes its own map as it goes.

The form of Christ in the world is therefore the way that the man of faith goes, in the society of faith; certainly, that is, in company with others, but not knowing whither he goes—except for this one certainty, that the way is the way of God and to God.

Prayer

These reflections, with their highly tentative and unspecific conclusions, their lack of conclusiveness or exclusiveness, and their subdued tones in contrast with the crass assurance of the fundamentalist and the brash self-confidence of those who declaim the burden of their own orthodoxy, will surely strike the activist spirit with dismay.

It is with him that I wish to speak now. With the fundamentalist, alas, and with the neo-orthodox, I can speak only tangentially—for they are far away from what I have tried to show is the central concern of a living Christian faith, the one with an idol of the past, the other with a packaged gospel which has been too long in the deep freeze of his own inner uncertainty.

Have we not, says the activist—have we not in Christian faith a whole catalogue of causes to be furthered, hopes to be realized, vindications of our decisions, which are to be made explicit in the tangle of warring objectives in our society? And if I say that we are not permitted as it were to lower our sights to these humbler objectives, then are we not denying, in the name of some nebulous other-worldliness, that very secularity which I have ushered in as the secular reality of Christ? How can this much-vaunted secular Christianity assume such a position of passivity? Am I not creeping back into the quietism and the a-sociality of so much of historical Christendom?

Nor is the entire substance of such objections concluded with these questions. For of course the activist spirit recognizes the necessity for a means of power, for a way by which he may activate his actions from outside of himself. He is perfectly ready, indeed he is anxious, to have guidance for his causes, whether he seeks that guidance in ecclesiastical pronouncements, or in a diligent searching of the scriptures, or in a combination of these means with his own intense longing for social justice, or the averting of nuclear war, or whatever his particular cause may be.

I hope it will not be considered unfair to illustrate the method of the average modern activist, of idealist or evangelical pretensions, by reference to its extreme form, even its caricature, in the writings of what have been called the practitioners of 'spiritual technology'.[1] Dr Hofstadter, in his admirable study of *Anti-Intellectualism in American Life* (a study which will probably never be paralleled in the less sophisticated British world), speaks of these practitioners as regarding religion as 'something to be used'.[2] Thus Norman Vincent Peale writes: 'If you will practise faith you can be healed of ill-will, inferiority, fear, guilt, or any other block which impedes the flow of creative energy. Power and efficiency are available to you if you will believe.' Or, in the words of Glenn Clark, 'A man who learns and practises the laws of prayer correctly should be able to play golf better, do business better, work better, love better, serve better.'[3]

Such illustrations may be useful, by their wellnigh unbelievable caricature of the reality of prayer, as a criterion for the general collapse of the understanding of prayer. For there can be little doubt that the ordinary view of the

[1]By Louis Schneider and S. M. Dornbusch in *Popular Religion: Inspirational Beliefs in America* (quoted by R. Hofstadter, *op. cit.*, p. 267.)
[2]Hofstadter, *op. cit.*, p. 265.   [3]*op. cit.*, p. 268.

professing Christian today vacillates between this brittle
optimism and an uneasy recourse to all manner of little
books about how to pray, manuals of unhappy naivety,
which quickly fall into desuetude, and are as quickly
replaced by more little books of the same kind. And the
end of this story is that the honest man gives up 'prayer'
altogether. It is probably not an exaggeration to say that
the vast mass of even conscientious church members have
entirely relinquished the habit of private prayer in any of
the conventional forms. And their adherence to the
practice of public prayer is linked with an increasing
distaste for being found in any place where they might be
exposed to the relics of this public practice. Bonhoeffer's
well-known remarks about his reluctance to use the name
of God in the presence of 'religious' people, joined with his
unwillingness to speak of God to those who have reached
the extreme of human suffering, Professor William Hamilton's moving confession, in *Thursday's Child*,[1] of his own
inability to form his life into a unity round the accustomed
styles of prayer, and Bishop John Robinson's provocative
formulation of the problem in his book, *Honest to God*,[2] all
indicate that we are facing here a crisis of the honest spirit,
which deserves every possible sympathetic attention.

The reasons for this general crisis lie deep in the theological crisis which has come upon the Christianity of our
time, and which is, indeed, the hidden occasion of the
present reflections. It is well to recall, however, that it was
St Paul who said, 'We do not rightly know what we are to
pray.' But in the same sentence he adds 'for the Spirit
has taken a hand in our weakness.' We are not able to
pray properly, but the Spirit looks after this. In other words,

[1]'Thursday's Child: The Theologian Between Today and Tomorrow', in *Theology Today*, January 1964.
[2]London, 1963. See esp. pp. 91–104.

our only recourse is the Spirit. This does not mean that we sit back and await a divine intervention. Rather, it means that we are thrown back into the historical situation which we would so gladly evade, if we could.

Prayer, therefore, is to be understood as the anticipation in the whole of our existence of that one End which is the reality of God. This does not mean that our recourse to the Spirit is the same thing as a spiritualizing of life. On the contrary, it means the presence in absence of the Spirit.

So prayer is not an attitude or a formula, it is not a content and not even a form. But it is the engagement of the whole life in the hope of the End in Christ. It is in the paradoxical union of the choice or the decision with the givenness of the End in Christ, of Christ as the Last Man, the foretaste and the promise, that prayer arises.

It takes forms, of course, and it has content too. But the forms and the content are determined solely by the union of the choice or decision with the givenness. Unless this choice and this longing recognition of givenness are present, there is no prayer.

But in the presence of this choice and this givenness prayer is not organized, or arranged: it simply happens, it is the being of the believer.

The manner, the style, the content, taken in and for themselves, are of the utmost insignificance. The anxieties which invade the simple believer's spirit concerning such matters of observance should be clearly defined: they are anxieties which belong not to the promised freedom of the spirit, but to the law. It is the givenness of the Spirit which alone counts: the Spirit 'helps our infirmity', and all the much-discussed problems of content, occasion, times and seasons, are less than irrelevant—they are delusive substitutes, and temptations which must be faced with courage.

Prayer must never be confused with its form or content.

'The Spirit intercedes for us.' 'He who knows the secrets of our heart knows also what is the intention of the prayers which the Spirit offers to God for us.'[1] Without this basic awaiting of the Spirit the forms of prayer are vacuous.

Only by way of the utter desolation of Christ's historical being on the Cross is prayer possible at all. It is thus the impossible possibility which is only found in the utmost mystery of the Spirit being with us and speaking for us. There is no place for anxiety if faith holds fast, in the power of the Spirit, hoping against hope, believing against unbelief.

So the conclusion is that the Spirit is the only power in the world. But this Spirit is power in powerlessness. 'Only a suffering God can help.'

[1]Romans 8.26-7.

BOOK LIST

INDEX

List of Books

ALTHAUS, P. *The So-called Kerygma and the Historical Jesus*, 1959, London

ALTIZER, T. J. *Mircea Eliade and the Dialectic of the Sacred*, 1963, Philadelphia

AUGUSTINE, ST. *The City of God*

BARTH, KARL *Kirchliche Dogmatik* III/2, III/3, Zürich; Eng. tr. *Church Dogmatics*, Edinburgh

BERKHOF, H. *Der Sinn der Geschichte*, 1962

BONHOEFFER, D. *Ethics*, 1955, London; Fontana ed., 1964
Widerstand und Ergebung, 1951, Munich; Eng. tr. *Letters and Papers from Prison*, 1953, London; Fontana ed., 1959

Bossey Ecumenical Institute Consultation on the Meaning of the Secular, 1959, Bossey, Switzerland

BRAATEN, C. E. and HARRISVILLE, R.A. ed. *The Historical Jesus and the Kerygmatic Christ*, 1964, London

BUBER, M. *I and Thou*, 1937, Edinburgh
Between Man and Man, 1947, London
Eclipse of God, 1952, London

BULTMANN, R. *Primitive Christianity*, 1956, London
Jesus Christ and Mythology, 1958, London
Jesus and the Word, 1960, London
History and Eschatology, 1959, Edinburgh
Glauben und Verstehen, 3 vols., 1933, 1952, 1960, Tübingen
Existence and Faith, 1961, London; Fontana ed., 1964

BUREN, P. VAN *The Secular Meaning of the Gospel*, 1963, London

COLLINGWOOD, R. G. *The Idea of History*, 1946, London

CULLMANN, O. *Christ and Time*, 1951, London

DIEM, H. *Dogmatics*, 1955, London

EBELING, G. *Wort und Glaube*, 1960; Eng. tr. *Word and Faith*, 1963, London
The Nature of Faith, 1961, London; Fontana ed., 1966

FRANK, E. *Philosophical Understanding and Religious Truth*, 1945, New York
Wissen, Wollen, Glauben, 1955, Chicago and Zürich
GODSEY, J. *The Theology of Dietrich Bonhoeffer*, 1960, London
GOGARTEN, F. *Ich glaube an den dreieinigen Gott*, 1926
Der Mensch zwischen Gott und Welt, 1956
Verhängnis und Hoffnung der Neuzeit, 1953
GRASS, H. *Ostergeschehen und Osterberichte*, 1956, Göttingen
HAMILTON, W. *The New Essence of Christianity*, London
HEGEL, G. W.F. *The Philosophy of History*, tr. J. Siebree, 1920, New York
HOFSTADTER, R. *Anti-Intellectualism in American Life*, 1964
HOLYOAKE, G. J. *Christianity and Secularism*, 1863, London
International Missionary Council, Jerusalem, 1928, London
JEAN PAUL *Siebenkäs*, 1796/7
JONAS, H. *Gnosis und Spätantiker Geist*, 2 vols., 1934, 1954, Göttingen
KÄHLER, M. *The So-called Historical Jesus and the Historic Biblical Christ*, tr. C. F. Braaten, 1964, New York
KIERKEGAARD, S. *The Last Years*, Journals 1853-5, tr. R. G. Smith, 1965, London
KÖRNER, J. *Eschatologie und Geschichte*, 1957, Hamburg
KUMMEL, W. G. *Das Neue Testament*, 1958, Munich
LEEUWEN, A. T. VAN *Christianity in World History*, 1964, London
LÖWITH, K. *Meaning in History*, 1949, Chicago
LÜBBE, H. *Säkularisierung*, 1965, Freiburg
MACINTYRE, J. *The Christian Doctrine of History*, 1957, London
MCINTYRE, J. *The Theological Frontier of Ethics*, 1961, London
MALET, A. *La Pensée de Rudolf Bultmann*, 1962, Geneva
MARXSEN, W. *Die Auferstehung Jesu als historisches und als theologisches Problem*, 1964, Gütersloh
MEYERHOFF, H. ed. *The Philosophy of History in our Time*, 1959, New York
MICHALSON, C. *The Rationality of Faith*, 1964, London
MOLTKE, H. J. VON *Letzte Briefe*, 1950, Berlin
MÜLLER, H. *Von der Kirche zur Welt*, 1961, Berlin
Mündige Welt, 4 vols., ed. Bethge E. 1955-63, Munich
NIEBUHR, H. R. *The Meaning of Revelation*, 1946, London
Christ and Culture, 1952, London
NIETZSCHE, F. *Fröhliche Wissenschaft*
OGDEN, S. M. 'The Temporality of God', in *Zeit und Geschichte*, ed. Dinkler, E., 1964, Tübingen

OMAN, J. *Grace and Personality*, 1917, 1960, London

RICHARDSON, A. *History Sacred and Profane*, 1964, London

ROBINSON, J. A. T. Honest to God, 1957, London
A New Reformation? 1964, London

SCHLATTER, A. *Das Christliche Dogma*, 1911

SCHWEITZER, A. *The Quest of the Historical Jesus*, 1922, London

SMITH, RONALD GREGOR *The New Man*, 1956, London
J. G. Hamann, 1960, London
'Theological Perspective of the Secular', *Christian Scholar*, March, 1960
'Post-Renaissance Man', in *Conflicting Images of Man*, ed., W. Nicholls, 1966, New York

STALLMANN, M. *Was ist Säkularisierung?*, 1960, Tübingen

SYMANOWSKI, H. *The Christian Witness in an Industrial Society*, 1964, Philadelphia; 1966, London

VAHANIAN, G. *The Death of God*, 1957, New York

WICKHAM, E. *Church and People in an Industrial City*, 1957, London

WINTER, G. *The New Creation as Metropolis*, 1963, New York

ZAHRNT, H. *The Historical Jesus*, 1963, London

Index of Biblical References

217

General Index

absoluteness, 20

action, Christian, 196, 204

action, of God, 117*ff.*; and his being, 119

Alaric, 69

Altizer, Thomas, 166

ambiguity, of secularism, 172

Anselm, 60, 61

apocalyptic, Jewish, 91, 113

archaeology, 72

Aron, Raymond, 82, 83, 85

aseity, God's, 120

assent, 44

attentiveness, willed, 35

Augustine, St., 60, 69, 73, 75*ff.*, 110

Averroes, 120

Barth, Karl, 15, 21, 32, 100, 102, 104, 115, 177, 202*f.*

Bentham, J., 144

Bernard de Ventadour, 179

Bible, and faith, 70

Bonhoeffer, Dietrich, 16, 32, 51, 150, 175*ff.*, 190*f.*, 200*f.*, 207

Bossey, 150

Buber, Martin, 44, 118, 123

Buddhism, 138

Bultmann, Rudolf, 27, 33, 36, 55*f.*, 80*f.*, 126, 128, 135, 151, 165

Caedmon, 74

Christ, relation of faith to, 47

Christendom, 194*f.*

Christianity: and faith, 26; and Gnosticism, 30*f.*

church, three forms of, 197

Clark, Glenn, 206

Collingwood, R. G., 71

creation, 40

Creed, Apostles', 45

criticism, emergence of biblical, 70*f.*

Cross, the, 92*f.*

crucifixion, and resurrection, 99

Cullmann, Oscar, 95*f.*, 113, 114

demythologizing, 33

dependence, 37

Descartes, R., 62

destiny, and fate, 42

directness, and faith, 62*f.*

docetic problem, 91, 137

Downing, Gerald, 27

dualism: in Christianity, 30; and gnosticism, 29*f.*; in theology, 120*f.*

Ebeling, G., 177

encounter, with otherness, 122*ff.*

eschatology, 50, 89*ff.*

existence, God's, arguments for, 59*ff.*

faith: Christianity as, 25*f.*; as commitment, 28; not empirical, 53*ff.*; and eschatology, 90*f.*; fruits of, 54*f.*; historicity of,